TENTH ANNIVERSARY VOLUME OF THE
MILLER CENTER OF PUBLIC AFFAIRS,
UNIVERSITY OF VIRGINIA

THE PRESIDENCY
AND
SCIENCE ADVISING

Edited by
Kenneth W. Thompson

UNIVERSITY
PRESS OF
AMERICA

Library of Congress Cataloging in Publication Data

The Presidency and science advising.

(Tenth anniversary series of the Miller Center of
Public Affairs, University of Virginia)
1. Science and state—United States.   2. Technology
and state—United States.   3. Scientists in government—
United States.   4. President—United States—Staff.
I. Thompson, Kenneth W., 1921-   II. Title:
Science advising.   III. Series.
Q127.U6P67   1986   338.97306   86-4132
ISBN 0-8191-5311-7 (alk. paper)
ISBN 0-8191-5312-5 (pbk. : alk. paper)

The views expressed by the author(s) of this publication do not
necessarily represent the opinions of the Miller Center. We hold to
Jefferson's dictum that: "Truth is the proper and sufficient antagonist
to error, and has nothing to fear from the conflict unless by human
interposition, disarmed of her natural weapons, free
argument and debate."

Co-published by arrangement with
The White Burkett Miller Center,
University of Virginia

All University Press of America books are produced on acid-free
paper which exceeds the minimum standards set by the National
Historical Publications and Records Commission.

Dedicated to
Dean Hugh P. Kelly
and
Professor Robert H. Kretsinger

Two Distinguished Scientists
who have inspired
and supported this
Miller Center Initiative

TABLE OF CONTENTS

PREFACE

The Miller Center of Public Affairs has sought to follow the injunction of a leading American philanthropist who declared: "In philanthropy as in baseball, you only score runs by bunching hits." Carried over into the study of public affairs, concentration is no less an appropriate working principle. Knowledge if it is to be cumulative must rest on colloquia and inquiries that mutually reinforce one another. Too often individual research proceeds on issues bearing no relationship to each other. Especially with social problems, such dispersion of effort tends to be the norm unless students and researchers can focus their energies on a common problem or an informing theory.

The Miller Center's common problem is the study of the American presidency. In choosing the presidency as its main focus, the Center has been faithful to the wishes of its donor. Mr. Miller was a Law School alumnus at the University of Virginia who sought to give back to his alma mater a donation from his substance that would make possible the establishment of a public affairs center. His particular concern was with the presidency and the problems which he saw in its functioning. Although he held strong personal views on such problems, he was content to see scholars of the future mark out fields of study which they considered urgent. He recognized with a former President of Brown University that "first class problems require first class minds" and such minds almost always are independent spirits.

The Miller Center has selected three broad areas for research and study on the presidency. The first has to do with particular presidencies. In this connection, we have conducted intensive oral histories of both the Ford and Carter White Houses. Another area for study has been the nature of the contemporary American presidency. Books have been published on the public philosophy and the presidency and the unwritten constitution. The third area concerned particular problems of the presidency and this area subsumes the Center's interest in the presidency and science advising. As we have sought advice and counsel on the most urgent problems of the presidency, this topic has repeatedly come to the fore. We have been encouraged by well-informed figures to make it an area of study at the Center.

Over the past two and a half years, we have conducted some half dozen Forums with distinguished scientists singularly well-qualified to discuss the major issues regarding science advising. We view these discussions as preliminary to a larger effort by the Center. Everyone who has addressed the problems of science advising from the standpoint of the presidency has described it as a neglected field of study. We have been encouraged to continue what we have begun and we would expect to do so. This volume is the first in what we expect will be a series of publications on the subject.

INTRODUCTION

The present volume is the product of Forum discussions with four quite different observers and practitioners in science advising. We have deliberately sought out scientists who represented different areas of professional competence and concern. Each of our speakers met with members of a colloquium who included natural and social scientists from the University of Virginia and retired public officials and community leaders. Their discussions were taped, edited by the speaker and recast in the form of publishable essays followed by questions and answers by Forum participants.

Early on, we encouraged a search for common themes. These included what is the role of the science adviser, who should play that role, what are the requirements for success and failure and what is the adviser's relation to the multiple constituencies he serves. Controversies have broken out regarding the location of the adviser in the government. Should his office be in the White House or outside? What about science advisers in Cabinet level Departments? How can the adviser avoid becoming a lobbyist for the science community or should he? What is the evidence that good science advising leads to better policy? Which Presidents have used science advisers most effectively?

The contributors to this volume are a longtime public servant, a political scientist, a Harvard physicist and a Princeton professor of Engineering. Each looks at science advising from a distinctive and different vantage point. Some of them differ fundamentally with one another. However, they reflect unanimity in the view that science advising is a vital and misunderstood aspect of the American presidency which no one has studied systematically.

Philip Smith is executive officer of the National Academy of Sciences and the National Research Council. Going back to 1973, he has served with three Presidents: Nixon, Ford and Carter. More than any other scientist, he has encouraged the Miller Center to make science advising an aspect of its research agenda. Through his efforts, the Center has made contacts with respected scientists especially concerned with the Office of Science and Technology Policy.

Ted Greenwood was a member of the MIT Department of Political Science when he spoke at the Miller Center but has since joined the faculty at Columbia University. Trained in physics as well as in political science, he is in the forefront of a small group of political scientists writing about science and technology. Not only are his studies of arms control and arms limitation known and respected, but he has a forthcoming book on the role of science and engineering knowledge in environmental health and safety regulation. His contribution to our volume is directed particularly to the requirements for effectiveness for the science adviser within the White House and the government.

Norman Ramsey is one of America's most renowned physicists. He is Higgins Professor of Physics at Harvard, past president of the American Physics Society and recipient of the Presidential Order of Merit for radar development work. Thanks to the initiative of Dean of Faculty and Commonwealth Professor of Physics, Hugh Kelly, Professor Ramsey while in residence at the University of Virginia Physics Department kindly appeared for a Forum at the Miller Center. He discussed science advising not only for the presidency, but the government as a whole.

Finally, Professor David Billington of the School of Engineering at Princeton presents the case for technology advising. His is a minority view in the present volume, but one deserving serious discussion. His thesis is that technology advice more nearly serves the practical and operational needs of the President and the White House. Scientists have tended to dominate in science advising circles but Billington questions whether their role has always been the most productive.

In bringing together the four viewpoints, the Miller Center intends only to open up discussion of the subject. We plan a continuing series of Forums and, if possible, specific research and writing projects.

THE PRESIDENCY AND SCIENCE ADVISING

Philip M. Smith

NARRATOR: In one of the presidential debates, President Reagan said "I'm not a scientist," and a good many Presidents could say that. Several of the visitors we had at the Miller Center who were close advisers, special assistants, to Presidents have said that one of the most difficult tasks they faced was in knowing which scientists to turn to and what kind of scientific advice to depend on with critical problems that have a large scientific component.

The Miller Center is a center for the study of the presidency, and from early in our period here we have felt that science advising to the

1

presidency was one of the most crucial issues. It is one in which, despite the presence of some of you at this table, we have limited competence at the Center. Political scientists are not known for their authority in the natural or physical sciences. Nonetheless it seems to be an area where there is a certain vacuum in the literature. One can point to a book of essays, there are memoirs and various writings, but neither by presidential scholars nor by scientists has there been a great deal of systematic study or analytic writing. Yet if a trillion-dollar program is to be the direction of the administration in the star wars area, obviously the need for the most objective and responsible science advising looms large.

So for all of these reasons we are very pleased to have Philip Smith with us this morning. From the very first time when we talked about this subject his name surfaced. Others who have spoken here or will speak are people like Ted Greenwood and Norman Ramsey. They have all mentioned Phil Smith. Indeed he has worked closely with Dick Merrill, the dean of our law school, and with several scientists who are around the table.

He is executive officer of the National Academy of Sciences and the National Research Council; he has served with three Presidents: Nixon, Ford, and Carter in the Office of Science and Technology Policy. He was a deputy to Frank Press; he has a scope and sweep of knowledge in the area going back to an appointment in 1973. Prior to that, he concerned himself in the National Science Foundation with research planning and research programs in the environmental sciences. He then worked in the Office of Management and Budget and had broad experience there. He is the author of a very significant study—in 1981—"The National Science Board and the Formulation of National Science Policy" which was a report to Lewis Branscomb, chairman of the National Science Board. He has played an important role in instituting a new journal which has already been quite successful, *Issues in Science and Technology.* Among the subjects in the current issue are "The Case for Ballistic Missile Defense" by George Keyworth, the President's science adviser in the current administration, and "The Case Against" by Sidney Drell and Wolfgang Panofsky.

Because of the long-standing importance of the problem, we are terribly pleased that Phil Smith has driven down from Washington as a gift to the Miller Center, and is joining us this morning to talk about the presidency and science advising.

MR. SMITH: Thank you. I am very pleased to be here and have a chance to chat with you. It is an interesting time to be talking about the presidency and science advising since we are in the midst of a presidential campaign. It is interesting to me that with the exception of two or three of these macro-technical issues, such as the President's proposed ballistic missile defense plan, research and development is not much of an issue in this campaign. There is, at least as we see it in Washington, a rather widespread consensus compared to times past about a great many of the features associated with policies for science, the role of the government in support of technology, and so forth.

I welcome the opportunity to talk with you. I've had a chance for a greater degree of reflection in the last couple of years than I did for quite a few years; thus I have thought more about the implications of what I did and my experiences in the whole decade of the seventies when I was fairly close to the presidential scene. Much of my commentary is actually drawn from a yet to be published paper that one of my former colleagues, Lawrence Linden, who is now at the McKinsey Company in New York, and I have been formulating. We are putting together I think a somewhat different view of the science adviser and the science advisory process. And that is what I am going to talk about today. I'll talk about a view that I strongly hold; I believe there is a need for a much broader discussion of the relationship between the science and technology advisory process in the presidency, and that it needs to be addressed much more from the perspective of the presidency than from the standpoint of the scientific and technical community, the principal commentators on the process up to this point in time.

I'll make only one or two comments about some historical issues. We can talk more about those in specific questions and answers if you want to talk about them. I will then describe my view of the operating environment of the science adviser and the reason why I believe that, except on rare occasion, the science adviser is always going to be a kind of a fourth tier player in the hierarchy of the presidency. I have some examples that I'll cite from the Carter presidency to illustrate some of these issues. And then I'll make one or two comments about what may lie ahead in the next few years.

Much of the discussion about science advising and the presidency has been from the standpoint of the scientific community itself. There has been very little analysis from the perspective of the presidential scholars who have been concerned about the growth of the modern presidency since Franklin Roosevelt. You look at most of the books that have been written, for example, even a book as recent as the book by Ben Heineman and Curt Hessler that was done somewhere around 1980, and the writings of people like Neustadt and so forth, and you see very little mention of the science advisory function. I think it must be viewed, debated and discussed much more from the standpoint of presidential scholarship. Science advice has to this point really been viewed mainly, in the presidential sense, as a constituency, that is, the expression of interests of science and technology community. This perspective by close advisors to Presidents has led to a number of interesting problems which have been associated with the function in the post-World War II period. However, if you view the function from the perspective of the presidency, as contrasted to the viewpoint of a scientist-advisor or the science community, you must conclude that this is going to be a dynamic, an ever changing, and an always unstable element of the Presidency. It is not going to be the kind of office that there is a good deal of aspiration for, particularly on the part of the academic science and engineering communities, who, as constituencies, hope for more than the science adviser process will ever be, except in cases of extreme or perceived technological threat.

The science community is basically much more informed today about the presidency and science advising than it was prior to the demise of the office in 1972. You remember that President Nixon, disenchanted for a variety of reasons with the presidential science adviser, abolished the office and relegated the function for a period of time to the director of the National Science Foundation. It was not until the very last part of the Ford presidency that the office became reinstated. The science community learned a lot about the presidency in that period but nonetheless as the discussion goes forward about the successes and failures of Dr. Stever, Dr. Press, and Dr. Keyworth as science advisers, one would have to say that the science and engineering communities are looking at this as an advocacy office rather than as an adviser and staff who understand the presidency and the integration of technical advice into the presidential decision-making process.

Part of the reason why this dilemma occurs is that there is an unnatural expectation arising from the one moment in which science and technology moved to center stage in the whole presidential structure. That was when we had the real or perceived missile crisis and technological threat from the Soviet Union in the Sputnik period. That was a technical emergency and a political emergency that has never since been repeated. Will we have again in the near future a similar kind of a technological emergency that will draw the science advisory process right into the center of the presidency in the sense that other White House activities are generally drawn in?

On the other hand the complexity of governance is constantly growing. Since that period of the Sputnik developments there has been an increased technological complexity of almost every presidential decision and there is a need for this kind of advice in the White House structure. And if the advice can be integrated in a way that it feeds into the variety of presidential activities and processes, it can play and should play a valuable role.

There are factors I would cite briefly which are behind my assertion that the science advisory process really needs to be viewed from the perspective of the presidency rather than the science and technology community.

For example, there has been and continues to be what can really only be described as a continued hand wringing about the relationship of science advisory activity and the presidency. There has been a great deal written on this in the science press. If you look at magazines like *Science* or *CNE News,* in every administration you see a lot of speculation about how frequently the science adviser visits with the President, and what kind of connections are visible from the symbols of photographs of science advisers with their Presidents and so forth. And whenever a novel or new reporting system has been constructed—as is the case, for example, in the current presidency wherein you have the triumvirate of central advisers: Baker, Meese and Deaver—immediately there is anguish within the science community as to what this implies for the presidential science adviser. Is he shut out formally from the process during the administration? Through whom does he report?

There is an unrealistic expectation of influence on the part of the scientific community as witnessed by the recurring debate about the office's organization. In 1980, for example, the scientific and technical transition team for the President was headed by the late Arthur Bueche, then group vice-president for research and technology at General Electric. His team recommended something that is possible under the legislation establishing the Office of Science and Technology Policy. They recommended a council of science advisers, a group of three persons, as compared to a single science adviser, the arrangement in preceding administrations. It was the principal recommendation of the Bueche transition team that there not be one but three science advisers. The expectancy was that if the science advisory process emulates the economic or the environmental process that somehow it will be better placed in the machinery of the presidency with a troika at the top to share the complex duties. I would contend that it was this recommendation made in 1980 that was one of the reasons why there was in fact something of a dilemma on the part of the President and his principal advisers as to what to do with the science process. As you recall it was some four or five months after the rest of the team got in place in January 1981 that Dr. Keyworth was appointed. He was appointed after several people had said no to an offer to serve in part because of this debate about expectancy, and a well understood rejection of it since staff memoranda rejecting the three adviser model had been circulated outside of the White House.

I have mentioned the nostalgia and the pining that goes on about the glory days when Sputnik was the crisis and we were as a nation inventing novel things, such as the reconnaissance satellite system that was developed in the late 1960s by the science adviser working for President Eisenhower. To show you how far we have come since that moment you should recall the first chapter of the report of the President's Science Advisory Committee. It was headed "Why Satellites Stay Up." It was a primer first lesson for President Eisenhower about why the Russians had gotten a satellite in orbit. It is this single period of advice that is the basis for the recurring overexpectation, and recommendations such as that proposing a Council of Science Advisers.

Another reason why there is a great deal of tension that again I think would support my assertion that we ought to look at the science office from the perspective of the presidency is tension between the overexpectation on the part of the Congress as to what this function ought to be, what the science adviser ought to do, and what the reality of the presidency is. There is no better example of this than the overreaching act that was created in 1976 when the Office of the Science Adviser was reestablished by legislative mandate. If you look at the first two titles of that act you see this long list of policies that the President's science adviser is supposed to implement, not only for the President but for also the Congress. And that is another important problem because of the separate powers of the branches.

There is within the Congress another factor. There is a continual push for overarching policy on virtually any topic, with implementation by the executive branch. The executive branch embodies pluralism and acts through incremental policy. In the area of Research and Development (R&D) there have been a series of events since the middle seventies that are illustrative of the kind of collisions that a President and his science adviser get into with the Congress. Two points of view are on a collision course in almost any technical or functional area you can think of. Strategic materials and minerals is a case in point, regulation of toxic substances is another.

Finally, there is this question of the President's science adviser as a cheerleader. It will always to some extent be the case that the President's science adviser is in fact the cheerleader for a constituency. But nonetheless if one is perceived too greatly by other advisers as a cheerleader one cannot really be a functional member of a presidential team. And the science community constantly flagellates itself over this matter. Thus, for example, when Dr. Keyworth in 1981 began talking about setting priorities in science and the fact that perhaps we cannot be first in every field he was reflecting the presidential perspective, or at least the perspective or constraint in the size of government. The academic community really desired advocacy of the science establishment of the country, not an advisory function for the presidency and thus was unprepared in some respects to hear Dr. Keyworth present his case.

Thus, for all of these reasons I feel very strongly that the Miller Center and other centers on the institution of the presidency, should foster more discussion about the function of science and technology advising. There could thus be a somewhat better balance than has come into this debate and discussion because it has principally been written about by scientists who are looking in from the outside in rather than people who are or have been on the inside looking out, or people who understand the whole breadth and reach of the presidential process.

I won't say much about history. Perhaps only three points. First, it is remarkable that only a few of the science advisers have written anything on this point. There is a very interesting diary by George Kistiakowsky, a dynamic document, in some respects illustrating how this all works. You read some interesting things about the relation between Kistiakowsky, the governmental coordinative processes, his relations with President Eisenhower, and so forth. Jim Killian has written a memoir of his time with Eisenhower. None of the more recent science advisers have yet written a great deal. One of the things that might be done at a place like the Miller Center would be to try to lure some of the advisers into the context of writing in a forum in which they would be more comfortable than writing in the scholarly science and technical journals where in effect they are writing for scientists rather than writing amongst people who are concerned with the presidential policy process. A few members of the science office staff in various presidencies have written accounts of their activity. But it is an interesting fact that there is by the science advisory community not all that much written.

Another important thing, I think, is that in all this discussion there has not been very much written, at least to my knowledge, about the function in the broader context of how things have gone in the United States—the currents. One doesn't see the function of the science adviser and the position's demise and reinstatement discussed in the context of the antiscience and antitechnology movement that developed in the late 1960s and the early part of the 1970s. At that time there was in fact in public perception quite a turn away from science and technology as a benefit to our society as compared to concern over a series of perceived threats from technology. People who have studied this matter, like Daniel Yankelovich, have some interesting things to say on attitudes about science, the public process, and the political process. I think it would be useful to have more commentary about the whole science advisory process from this standpoint because the broader social and political attitudes really need to be understood.

Finally, there are a lot of structural developments bearing on the advisory process that have taken place. These also need to be taken into account. If you think about the differences in presidential science advising between 1965 and 1985 you have to think about the following. In 1965 there was an office in the White House and there was a fairly strong coordinative function amongst the federal agencies. This was the Federal Council for Science and Technology. The Congress itself was not fitted out with much technical advice of any kind. There was, to be sure, the Congressional Research Service, but the offices that are now in place to directly assist the Congress—the greatly expanded General Accounting Office that does technical audits as well as financial audits, the Office of Technology Assessment, the Budget Office—none of those were in place.

Think tanks increasingly are doing contracted technical work for various departments and agencies so you find a broad array of people for hire, so to speak, to provide technical advice at all levels of the government, particularly for the offices of the White House, not only the science office but the other offices of the White House as well.

There are interesting developments in institutions like the Brookings Institution and the American Enterprise Institute. Particularly at the moment the American Enterprise Institute is doing some very interesting work in technology, international competition, international trade, and so on, and has in fact begun to take up the analysis of technical and scientific issues. I think all of these structural changes that have taken place need to be thought about as one thinks about the science advice and the presidency.

Now a few words about the presidential operating environment, as I call it. There are, as I see it, five kinds of processes or centers of activity in the presidency. If the science adviser is going to be successful he somehow has to get hooked into four of these five processes because he and his office represents the fifth of the five processes that I consider to be the principal processes of the presidency. The science adviser is seen by others as being a member of this fifth group.

First, there are the immediate personal, political advisers. Every President equips himself with a few such individuals who are in effect, to be blunt about it, the gatekeepers. They are the people who control the agenda of the President, the access to the President, deal with the political sensitivities, attempt to try to fulfill the campaign pledges, and so forth. We have had a series who are well known: Joe Califano in the Johnson presidency; Haldeman and Ehrlichman in the Nixon presidency; Hamilton Jordan, Jody Powell, and to some extent Stuart Eizenstat in the last presidency; and of course Baker, Deaver, and Meese, a triumvirate that were the central gatekeepers in the first Reagan term.

Now the President's science advisers, except for the case of Kennedy and his adviser, Jerome Wiesner, have had to earn their way in through the gate. Except for Wiesner, there have been no presidential science advisers who have started with a close relationship with the President or with the gatekeepers. So it is not a foregone conclusion, even if you are an eminent scientist or engineer and you come to the front door and knock, that you are going to be allowed in. You have to earn your way in. That's the first set of advisers that the science adviser has to cope with. Naturally there are a lot of other people around the White House structure who are trying to earn their way in also so you are in effect in competition with all the other people who want to get on the President's agenda.

The second group of activities which the science adviser must associate himself with is the broad, integrating policy staffs of which there are really three, but one of them is a unique one, the Office of Management and the Budget (OMB), and I'll come to OMB in a moment. These policy staffs are the National Security Council staff and the Domestic Council staff. In various incarnations these two groups have been in place over most of the post-World War II presidency. The NSC of course dates from the Truman presidency and although there are various ups and downs in its success, it remains a very powerful policy integrating force within the presidency. And the science adviser, in effect, if he is going to have a full range of activity in which he can play useful, technical advisory roles, has to get hooked up with the national security process. It is hard to do.

One of the first things I did when we were talking about all of this at the beginning of the Frank Press period was to point out that we had to find some way to get into this process. In the Kissinger NSC period before he went to the State Department there was an enormous growth of the NSC. Because of the vacuum created by the abolition of the science advisory process in the White House, there was a great growth in the technical competency of the NSC. In order to reenter that process, it seemed to me, we had to devise some special ways of having access. So we concocted an arrangement that turned out to be rather effective. We had on our staff one of my colleagues in that period, Ben Huberman, who worked on national security matters. He had worked on them in earlier presidencies. We arranged a joint appointment for him, both on the NSC staff and in the Science Advising staff and thus he was a double-hatted and human link between these two functions. It provided a way for us to work on a host of issues that we would not have been able to work on otherwise because we would have in effect been shut out of some parts of the national security process.

The same goes for the domestic policy process. Since domestic activity really is the physical embodiment and manifestation of the President's agenda as most people in the United States think about it, those people are very political, very sensitive to the issues. The legitimacy of these people as advisers is total in the domestic arena, and you have to find your way into that realm as a science adviser.

The third group of players in the White House are the owners of powerful presidential processes. I would cite two. The first and the most powerful of course is the budget process. It is an integrating and policy activity, but more. It is the most remarkable function of the government. And although it has had many permutations and ups and downs over the years, it remains to this day the single most remarkable presidential process. And there has been nothing developed by the Congress in its efforts since 1974 to emulate the executive capacity. So the budget adviser remains a process owner of great moment and you must play in that arena if you are going to be a successful science adviser. That is not necessarily a foregone conclusion, although there is a tendency on the part of some budget directors to relegate some aspects of the budget, funding for science itself and for agencies like the National Science

Foundation, to the science adviser. There is, nonetheless, an inherent suspicion on the part of the budgetary leaders that the science adviser really is a constituency representative, and that he will always come out on the side of spending more rather than spending less when it comes down to a choice between dollars for basic research or dollars for a social program. You run into a lot of interesting things in this respect.

We developed a three hundred million dollar add-on for science at one point in one of the budgets in the late seventies and we were in the process of distributing this—it was for basic research—to try to balance certain areas where the budget would benefit from new initiatives in basic research. We ran into a Cabinet officer who was somewhat apathetic toward research and development. When presented with the idea of having another twenty million dollars, he said to the deputy director of the budget, "I don't want it." So the deputy director of the budget called up the president's science adviser, Frank Press, and said, "He doesn't want it," and Press said, "Well, that's too bad." And the next thing that the deputy director said was, "You're not going to make me give it to him even if he doesn't want it, are you?" If the science adviser had at that point said yes, that would have been probably the end of the credibility of the science adviser with the deputy director of OMB in the remainder of that presidency, or as long as the two incumbents were in place.

The other process owner who is important owns the presidential appointment process. And this is important from the perspective of the President's science adviser. In fact the appointments to the various R&D positions in the government are critically important as appointments to the advisory boards and commissions. That is a process in which the advisers over the seventies—Ed David, Guy Stever, Frank Press—played with a remarkable degree of success. It has been a little more difficult for Dr. Keyworth to play in this arena, I think, in part because of the extreme ideological imprimatur that has been put on the appointment process by some of the people working for the President. So Dr. Keyworth has had a great deal of frustration in dealing with this group of people. But they are again the owner of an important process, and if you can't work your way into that process and somehow gain their confidence, your capacity to influence the appointment of various positions is damaged.

The President's science adviser oftentimes can win in critical appointments at the early part of an administration. That was of course another one of the problems about the long delay in the appointment of Dr. Keyworth. At the beginning of Dr. Press's time he took exception with a couple of Cabinet officers about their proposed appointments and won by in effect saying to the President and to his personnel director, "This individual is not suited for the management of agency X under this department, and if you appoint a person of this kind you are not going to bring credit to your administration. You are in effect going to illustrate the fact that your leadership really doesn't understand what the R&D departments of the government are all about and how to appoint the kind of people who ought to be placed into them."

The fourth set of players in the White House and around the presidency are the institutional advisory staffs. The science office is one of these. The others are the environmental office, the economic office, and the similar offices that are legislated. Of these the Council on Economic Advisers is the player of longstanding. Much has been written about it. From the perspective of the presidency the science adviser has to be examined in this light, among others, because the Office of Science and Technology Policy is a kind of an institutionally mandated function. It is a focused function just as the economic adviser is, the environmental adviser, and so forth. The institutional advisers are inevitably, except in rare cases—the economic adviser has certain connections that are a little bit different—basically advisers who, except when there is a special problem, are at the fourth tier of the hierarchy of presidential advising, behind the gate keepers, the integraters, and the process owners.

Finally, there are all the other players within the White House structure. In any presidency there is a desk officer for almost any kind of thing. You have an intergovernmental affairs adviser; you have an inflation fighter in some moments when inflation is rampant; you have people who attend to minorities; you have people who attend to religious groups. This panoply of people are around. Occasionally you can build interesting alliances with one or the other of these that can be useful to the President and useful from the perspective of the science adviser. Over the 1970s, the intergovernmental adviser was fairly influential in successive presidencies. There were some alliances that began to develop, for example, on work that we did on the question of productivity, inflation, innovation, and international competitiveness as viewed with the growing competition with Japan and so forth that involved a number of these specialist or desk officer advisers as well as others such as the domestic adviser and his staff.

The science adviser relates also to the executive departments and Congress. The Cabinet departments, you know, are part of the presidency, but also they are not. Every President starts off with a strong commitment to Cabinet government. By the end of the second year the President and his main advisers are beginning to view the Cabinet officers in a different light: victims of constituents and of the committees of the Congress that govern their appropriations and authorizations in the annual march to the Hill for dialogue with the Congress. The Cabinet and the independent agencies present for the science adviser a particular set of challenges. On the one hand there are a lot of cross-cutting governance issues in science and technology that are not well attended to unless they are attended to by the President's science adviser. On the other hand if you are too closely allied with this set of players you begin to limit your access to the presidential advisers because you are viewed as being in consort with people whose loyalties to the President have diminished over the time that they have been in office because they are increasingly spokespersons for their constituency, be it transportation, be it health, be it defense, whatever. So that is a factor that a science adviser has to contend with.

The Congress, of course, viewed from this perspective and not from the viewpoint of the Congress, is an array of fractionated committees and subcommittees that can advance their own agenda by attaching themselves, in one way or another, onto the coattails of the science adviser and others in the presidency. Thus you have a recurring effort, for example, on the part of the science committees in the House and the Senate to reopen the debate about a national science policy. The chairman of the House Science and Technology Committee has announced just recently that all of the next Congress is going to be, in their committee, devoted to another examination of national science policy. It is less than ten years since the last such debate took place. This creates an enormous amount of tension because these congressional committees and subcommittees come up with a variety of unrealistic expectations. In the last days of the recently concluded Congress, for example, I can think of seven or eight pieces of authorizing legislation that set up new requirements for the President's science adviser to do this or that. For example, to be a member of an Arctic research commission, set up a new critical materials advisory board, etc. You find this stuff written into the back part of congressional bills. And of course if the science adviser attempts to take care of these interest activities he has little time for anything else and little credibility as a member of a presidential team.

So in summary I would say the operating environment is dynamic.

The science adviser is never really part of the first team or the second team because he is not a political adviser and he doesn't own a powerful process like the budget process. And only when there is this rare case in which the science adviser moves to the front stage do you have this kind of growth of authority. And so the adviser's effectiveness varies on any given issue.

The political prominence of the issue is important. That of course was the thing that connected Killian and Eisenhower together in such a central way. We had the perceived technological threat from the Soviet Union that was in effect a national political emergency. How were we going to combat the Soviet ICBM and Sputnik capacity? Whether there will be any such emerging issue in the late 1980s is an interesting thing to think about.

The more science there is in an issue, the heavier the adviser's role. That does not necessarily mean that the same thing pertains for technology. Other advisers have a bigger handle on technology questions associated with the presidency. For example, when you get into something like synthetic fuels, you get into a lot of issues that have economic considerations. If you get into some of the regulatory questions that have to do with risk assessment, you have a lot of players and you have a lot of economic and political considerations as well as scientific considerations. So when you get into those kinds of questions, the dominant role of a science adviser is less.

The President's respect for the science adviser is very important. If you earn your way and if the President calls on you on a regular basis, you can increase your capital amongst the other advisers. For example, if a President, in the Cabinet room during a budget process or a Cabinet meeting will in effect have a long dialogue with the science adviser about a matter, the Cabinet officers, begin to notice and pay attention. We did an interesting thing early in the Carter presidency. Because of President Carter's interest in the future capacity of the nation that would come from basic research, we got a memo around to the Cabinet officers about this subject. And that was a signal to everybody that the President had an interest in science and respected his science adviser.

Perceived loyalty as seen by the other advisers is very important. This goes up and down on the basis of a lot of the factors I've mentioned.

Then there is the question of the utility of the science adviser. There are a lot of things about the presidency that are essentially best described as dealing with messy problems of governance. Nobody in a presidency really likes to spend any time on them because they are often intractable.

They involve the jurisdictional fights amongst departments and agencies. They involve problems that are not immediate; they are problems that are of a longer term character. And many of them have a technological component. If a science adviser is willing to take on issues of this kind he will grow in stature amongst his colleagues on the White House staff because he is seen as a team player, a utility infielder so to speak.

Now let me just mention briefly a few more examples that illustrate the presidential structure. I mentioned the matter of dealing with the appointments process in the Carter presidency and taking on a couple of Cabinet officers about their appointments. That was a risk in one sense of the word because all could have been lost right off the bat in the early days of the administration if there had been some kind of a showdown and the presidential science adviser had lost. It would have done quite a bit of damage to the future power base of the science adviser that had to be thought about at the time of the intervention.

The budgets are important. Dr. Keyworth has been remarkably successful in dealing in this arena. His two predecessors also had a strong influence on the budgetary process, and this largely came from creating allies and alliances with the budgetary advisers. And that is a process in which the presidential science adviser's staff plays an important role. Technical competency is valuable in the budgetary analysis and the decisions that have to be made. But you have to have the capacity to work through all of the endless analysis that goes on and the endurance to stay in the process.

Energy is an interesting problem as it is reflected in the last two administrations, particularly the Carter administration. The President's Science Adviser Office was not all that influential in the energy area largely because the issues at hand were often not technical questions. There were to be sure technical questions associated with various options and alternatives for future power supplies such as synthetic fuels, solar energy, and so forth. But for the most part the discussion about energy had to do with macro-economic conditions and national political strategies. Therefore the role of the science adviser and the Office of Science and Technology Policy was really remarkably limited. And there was no participation, for example, in that great discussion that went on at Camp David in which the President came down later and addressed the nation about national malaise. He did arrange a special briefing on technologies for the president but the science advisory process was absent in all that discussion about what was wrong with America and most of the broad questions of energy policy.

Moreover, there were oftentimes in the energy area disagreements that in effect put the science adviser in opposition to other advisers. The goal, for example, that was espoused by President Carter of having twenty percent of the national energy derived from solar energy by the year 2000 is technically and economically unrealistic. It was and is. He indicated that. There was enormous pressure by the other advisers to have our contrary view changed. One by one the other advisers, came into Frank Press's office and said, "Please change your view about this because you are the single dissenting vote." And Dr. Press said, "My job is to provide technical advice. Others provide other kinds of advice, I'm not going to change my vote. The President will understand what I am talking about. He has to make the decision on the basis of broader considerations that include but are not limited to my advice!" So energy represented in this matrix of presidential power an interesting illustration of the relation of science adviser and other presidential advisers.

Let me cite still another energy issue to illustrate my aforementioned points. Nuclear power as a subset of energy was interesting. Deterrence of the proliferation of weapons was very high in the last administration's priorities. It still is an important problem but it has not been as high on the agenda of this President as it was in the last presidency. A curious event took place early in the Carter administration. It was assumed on the part of the other advisers that the technical adviser would be an advocate for nuclear energy and therefore there was a suspicion about including the adviser and his staff in the non-proliferation discussions because there was a feeling that we would be strongly in favor of nuclear power, the free interchange and movement of nuclear materials for commercial nuclear power, and so forth. Some of the other advisers and staffs, particularly the domestic adviser or the environmental adviser, were absolutely certain in their construction of science advice that we would come out on the "wrong" side of this issue. Therefore they cut us out early in the administration and we did not have a big role in the early days. A non-proliferation role grew in time.

On the other hand, a problem such as high-level radioactive waste management, one of the messy problems of government, as I describe them, that doesn't seem to get resolved from one decade to the next, was a problem that the other advisers were quite happy to consign to the science adviser. In fact we spent the greater part of a four-year period creating the strategy that was finally enacted by the Congress in 1982. There was in that problem plenty of willingness to let the science adviser work the issue.

When we had the Three Mile Island episode, the President took his science adviser to Pennsylvania but did not take the director of the Nuclear Regulatory Commission along. That was a kind of political symbolism.

Other problems that have fallen into the hands of the science adviser recently are things like earthquake hazards. After the Mount St. Helen's explosion, the President asked Dr. Press what would happen if we had a major earthquake in California. Well, it turned out that not all that much thought had been given to what would happen. In all probability there will be a major earthquake in California in the next fifteen or twenty years. We discovered a lot of interesting things. For example, the tracking station which was critical to the reconnaissance satellite system was abreast of the San Andreas fault. So you can be a utility infielder on these messy, technically complex issues and by so doing you can increase your capital amongst the other presidential advisers.

I want now to make one other point before concluding with some comments about the future of the science advisory function. In some presidencies there may be one or two unforeseen developments which become an opportunity for the science adviser to play a major, perhaps even an historic role. If an advisor can respond effectively, his influence may be profoundly important in the broadest political sense. That, after all, was the role Killian played.

The Carter China initiative is a case in point. You will recall that in 1978 the President's security adviser and science adviser went to China, and in fact took the second step—the first step being the trip of Henry Kissinger and President Nixon—in opening up the broader relations with the People's Republic of China. The technical, scientific, and commercial relationships became the framework for further normalization. It was an interesting case where scientific and technical issues fitted together very well with the presidential interest and our national security interest. There was a close linkage of the science advisor to the presidency.

Let me close by posing some thoughts about the future of the advisory function. I think there are some interesting issues to think about today and as one thinks about the late 1980s. There is today a remarkable consensus between the parties and between the executive and the congressional branches about R&D. The kinds of things that even ten years ago were discussed in the Congress about the utility of basic research are no longer subjects of conversation. Twenty years ago when I was working at the National Science Foundation we went through an annual congressional exercise in which we were describing in answers to questions the following: How does one know when one has done enough basic research? Now you don't have that kind of conversation going on nor do you have the kind of thing that went on in the years of the Golden Fleeces, or the members of the Congress, in the House especially, who would get up and talk about grant titles that they thought embodied the wastefulness of money going into basic research.

However, this consensus does not hold in the area of the private and public sector relationships in applied research and technology for national needs, for example energy development. There is no consensus, and that is an area where there needs to be a great deal of public and private sector discussion in the years ahead. We have not found our way here. If you look at what has transpired since the early 1970s in the way of starts and stops in various initiatives you find that we are still faltering. Some would contend that getting our act organized in this area is a necessary step toward our being in a better position to compete with our international competitors and allies, like the Japanese.

Another important change that needs to be considered is that the states are taking up a renewed interest in science and technology, the support of research at the state level, the rebuilding of education, the creation of various centers of one kind or another to spur the linkages between universities and industry and set up innovation and so on. There has long been at the federal level a kind of perspective held by some that somehow we needed to transfer the benefits of the federal investment more fully into the state and local processes. Top-down pushes of one kind or another over the years have not succeeded in doing very much to get that to happen. But consider what is going on right now: what Governor Robb, for example, is doing here; Governor Hunt in North Carolina; Governor Bond in Missouri; and Governor Babbitt in Arizona. Governors and state legislatures are deeply involved in these questions of science and technology. I think from the perspective of the future of the science advisory function and the presidency this is an important matter to be thought about.

Industry's own role is also interesting. Industry in the United States is now spending upwards of sixty billion dollars on research and development. The private sector expenditures exceed the federal expenditures, including the federal expenditures for defense. Thus you see remarkable things. A company like DuPont, for example, is spending one billion dollars this year on R&D of which a quarter (two hundred and fifty million dollars) is directed toward their new ventures: pharmaceutical, life sciences, agriculture, all centered in genetic engineering. One company after another is building linkages with universities and creating a kind of a new enterprise that did not exist over the sixties and seventies when the federal government was the principal player and patron in the support of research in universities.

These kinds of questions lead to the issue of how best to manage R&D in the late 1980s from the federal perspective. What should the relationship of the adviser and the President be? Some contend perhaps that we should revisit the question of a Department of Science and Technology. Dr. Keyworth himself has proposed that perhaps the time has come for such a Cabinet enterprise. It has been thought about many times by members of Congress and by Cabinet officers in times past. Presumably if one created a department, that action would relieve the adviser of a lot of his or her coordinative functions where you are involved in the governance and the management of the R&D function of the government as compared to advising the President.

In light of a department, what kind of an office and what kind of an advisory structure would remain? It presumably would be a function that would be completely directed toward working on technical questions of presidential interest. Whether that kind of configuration will emerge in a future presidency after 1985 or not is hard to say.

But whatever happens I would contend that the office will essentially have to recreate itself, the function will have to recreate itself, in every future presidency just as it has in past presidencies and the President will have to discover the kind of relationship he wants to have with his technical adviser and vice versa.

If there is any one thing going for the science adviser function it is not all of the aspiration of the scientific community, the rhetoric in the engineering community about the need for more engineering, or the views or the aspirations of the Congress. It is this alone: the technical and scientific interplay in the presidential decision process is evermore present, evermore complicated, and it will always be harder. Occasionally it is a direct, central feature of the presidential process and the presidential decisionmaking. It is almost always present to some degree, greater or lesser in almost everything the President is thinking about in the modern presidency. And if the science advisory function can be properly understood and embedded into the process I think it can serve a useful role in the future as it has in times past.

QUESTION: I wanted to ask two questions related perhaps to the two themes you concluded with. One thing I think has become quite obvious from many of the past discussions is the question of style. Each President has his or her own style. To what extent can the process of scientific and technical advice be adapted to the style of each President? To what extent can it be institutionalized? And related is the question of whether there is or could be such a thing as scientific and technical policy as opposed to the impact of scientific and technical advice on defense policy, on environmental policy, etc.? How realistic is it to think of a science policy regardless of where it emanates from?

MR. SMITH: Well, in answer to the first question, style is important in addition to the institutional dynamics. Different science advisers have come from different backgrounds. Dr. Keyworth, of course, is notably unlike his predecessors in terms of previous experience and background. His experience was largely in national laboratory activity and the defense arena. He had not been active in national societal affairs of science to the extent that most of his predecessors had been. He had not been associated with universities. He also came in late, after the train had left the station so to speak. He was appointed in May or June after that first round of budgetary activity that Mr. Stockman had begun and was faced with quite a dilemma. And in some respects I have always felt that some of the rhetoric, the style, that he adopted, which sounded very strident from the standpoint of the research community in academia, was in fact a necessity on his part in order to be a member of the team at that moment at a time in which "giving at the office as well as giving at home" was the mode of life around the White House. Those who gave the most were the ones who in effect were seen by the President as being the most patriotic and the most loyal. So he started talking about priorities, a need to make cuts, and suggesting that not every field of science would get growth. There was discussion about a twenty percent cut in funds for basic research and so forth. There was a necessity on his part to try to prove himself.

Style is always going to be important. That in itself would be, I think, the subject of a good piece of writing about the presidency and the science advisory process. The people who have done a lot of cataloging do not really get to the subtleties of that kind of issue. Kistiakowsky was rather reserved in describing any of his own thinking or his relationships. Probably Killian's book describes a little more of this. I think that is an interesting question and one that would be almost worthy of a seminar in itself.

Now with regard to science policy, I guess my view is, and this is strictly my own view, that the only real embodiment of science policy is and always will be the direct support of research and the conditions and mechanisms necessary for research; that's science policy. Everything else is essentially technological or it is a function of defense policy, environmental policy, regulatory policy in either the economic or the health, worker safety, environmental sense. Those functions of the President's science adviser that are in support of science—the budget, the appointments, trying to work out some of the intractable regulatory problems of research like indirect costs, effort reporting—those are the elements of science policy. The rest of the office and its activity is very much tied into all this other array of presidential activities. I think the science and engineering community would be more helpful and supportive of an incumbent science adviser if it thought a little more about the distinction between these two very different roles of the President's science adviser.

NARRATOR: It shows the value of an interdisciplinary effort that the chairman of biology should ask the question on political styles.

QUESTION: Most of the science you talked about, especially in relationship to engineering technology, sounds pretty much like physical science. The health sciences and the concluding behavioral sciences you haven't mentioned much about, as far as the input into that office and, secondarily, an input into the President and yet when you talk about OMB you did mention the NIH, the National Institutes of Health budget. I wonder if you could talk a little bit about how that kind of advice gets to the President.

MR. SMITH: I should have mentioned it. That's a good question; I'm glad you brought it up. It illustrates one of these major changes that has taken place in the office and its activity. If you look at the Killian and Kistiakowsky memoirs you see that almost everything in their range of activity was associated with physical sciences and engineering. Kistiakowsky described one or two episodes of a health character. I think that during his time we had that FDA episode with cranberries in which the cranberries were contaminated and it was an issue that he played a role in. I think there was a red dye, a food coloring additive problem that he got involved in. In that whole period of time clear on up into the Kennedy presidency, the science advisers, except in the concern for the agencies like the NIH, didn't really deal very much with environmental, health, or biological kinds of issues.

Edward Burger who worked in the Nixon-David period wrote a book about his activity on the last of the Presidential Science Advisory Committee reports. I think the title of his book was *Science at the White House*. That period was the beginning of change. If you look at the titles of the Presidential Science Advisory Committee reports you see that all the whole first two-thirds of them dealt with physical, technical, and engineering kinds of issues, such as defense and national security and with education. Then you see energy, risk assessment, health questions, issues associated with diet and nutrition and so forth beginning to show up. The late 1960's brought health into the science advisory activities.

During the interregnum, when there was no office in the White House, Dr. Stever had a broader range of activities in the health and biological area perhaps partly because of the base of support of the National Science Foundation (NSF). We reinstituted the office into the White House in 1976, we divided the responsibilities into health and biological activity; energy, basic science, and general government; and, national security and international affairs, each supervised by an associate OSTP director. And so in that period and on through the end of the Carter presidency there was quite a lot of interplay of the science adviser and his staff on technical and on risk assessment issues. There are some now. One of Dr. Keyworth's deputies, Bernadine Buckley, is involved in the interagency group that is looking at what to do about the question of regulating genetic engineering. There is a revision of the national cancer plan that Dr. Keyworth's office has been involved in.

This question illustrates one of the dilemmas that you run into when you talk to the old-timers who were part of the presidential science advisory committee. They complain bitterly about the fact that there is not now a presidential science advisory committee. The dynamics of the presidency, as you know, tend to shuck those sorts of things off because they are appendages around the presidency. Every President likes to try to get rid of these committees.

But the legitimate question is: Can you assemble one team of six or eight people, or ten people, to be an advisory group that can deal with the range of issues that one now has to deal with of a technical character? One of the things that went wrong, frankly, with the President's Science Advisory Committee in its later days was that you had people speaking outside areas of their competency. Thus you had, for example, in the question of automobile emissions, the first round of discussion in the late sixties and early seventies before the catalytic converter settlement with the three auto companies took place, committees who were largely physicists and engineers essentially serving in an analytical process that was largely a process of understanding a lot of questions of health and risk, lifetime exposure, economic and private sector management and so forth. If you were to have a presidential science advisory committee today, what group of ten or twelve wise men or women would you assemble who could cover the broad range of technical issues?

QUESTION: Dr. Smith, you covered to some extent policy and the immediate messy problems. Is it reasonable and useful that the President have specific but broad objectives in the field of science and technology?

MR. SMITH: Well, that's the hope of the Congress, of course. In the legislation that reestablished the office there was the aspiration that somehow the presidential science adviser would be a voice, a spokesperson, for longer-range goals.

There is a small but growing body of literature about strategic planning in the presidency, and the fact that it doesn't take place. That's the bottom line, I think. Various configurations that have been tried in the modern presidency from the Roosevelt days forward to try to organize a method for long-range planning and the enunciation of goals as a process of the presidency have tended not to work for a host of reasons. It is hard to get a long range kind of a process positioned amongst all of the other forces at work without the planning becoming captured by one or another sector. And then there is a question of whether you can plan out of the context of political considerations and the political mandate of the President. It is a real dilemma. There is the pressure of time and the immediate. We answer the phone that had the immediate issue at the other end as compared to the phone call about the longer range issue because that is the way life is near the political center.

So I don't know whether planning in the sense of this discussion can be ever embedded in the presidency very well. The time horizons of the presidency, the time horizons of the corporate sector, the time horizons of other public officials, the Congress and so forth are really three to five years for a variety of reasons. I think that nongovernmental entities play a much more valuable role in thinking out the longer term agenda: organizations like Brookings, the Urban Institute, AEI, my own organizations—the National Academy of Sciences and the National Research Council—the new academic centers such as the one at Harvard on health policy, and university centers concerned with public policy, the presidency, and so forth.

The discussion and debate about the longer term, at least right now, is going to be better advanced by these kinds of institutions than is going to be done by any kind of an advisory process or an individual adviser inside the White House. You just don't have any time to deal with the longer term. You don't have time to read. All you read is what you are going to talk from tomorrow morning when you go up to the Hill and testify. You don't read books or analytical kinds of documents, and so forth. It is a real firefighting kind of operation so you don't get long-range planning under way too well in the context of the presidency.

In our country we've been preoccupied with the Japanese success for the last six or eight years. Japanese processes have been subject to a lot of analysis—for example, MITI, the Ministry for Industry and Technology. They have a kind of national planning process, the likes of which you can never imagine implanting in our system because of the diverse, pluralistic nature of our government and our society. So to organize a kind of a central planning function or even a presidential strategic planning function that reaches a long way out seems pretty hard, to my way of thinking, to imbed in either the science office or in the presidency itself.

Every President complains about not getting enough long-range advice and of being captive to the moment. But long term planning doesn't seem somehow to find its way into the processes. Some Presidents gather longer term views together from individuals coming and going through their office. One of the things that Frank Press did on occasion was to get interesting people in to see President Carter. President Ford did the same thing on occasion with Dr. Stever. In terms of information transfer, this kind of human information transfer probably is a more successful means of getting something done than trying to have a process.

NARRATOR: We thank you for launching our inquiry into the "President and Science Advising" in a quite remarkable and searching way.

SCIENCE AND TECHNOLOGY ADVICE FOR THE PRESIDENT

Ted Greenwood

NARRATOR: The comments that over the years I remember hearing about Professor Greenwood at MIT from political scientists like Bill Kaufmann and George Rathjens were that he was the best that there was in a very small population of political scientists who write about science and technology.

Early on, Ted Greenwood made science and technology an area of major concern. His early book on the effect of new scientific and technological developments as they interacted with the development of MIRV was widely heralded as an attempt, and a successful one, to bring to bear new scientific and technological knowledge that helped to illuminate the problem of arms development and arms control. He discussed scientific but also strategic questions that grew out of the development of MIRV.

He is trained in physics as well as in political science with degrees from MIT. He quickly established himself as one of the most successful and respected professors on the MIT faculty and developed a wide following of students at that institution. He has worked in the area of arms control and arms limitation. He also has had a continuing interest in science policy, science and technology and international relations. That dual interest is unique in the field of political science where the choice so often seems to be one or the other rather than coverage of the breadth of the field. He served for two years under Dr. Frank Press in the office of the President's science advisor (OSTP). He has served in other capacities in Washington. So he has put his interest in science and technology to work in a public service capacity. He has a forthcoming book on the role of science and engineering knowledge in environmental, health and safety regulation. He is also working in the arms control area, particularly at the moment on conventional deterrence in the NATO southern flank area, intending to use the topic as a wedge to illuminate wider subjects of arms control as well. This is a strategy parallel to his move a decade ago into the energy field with a Canadian study as a prime subject of attention as a kind of opening into the broad energy field.

As several of the scientists around the table know, we have talked for a long time about whether or not, in a center concerned with presidential studies, there was any role for the Miller Center to play in the study of the President's science advisor system. Various organizational patterns have been followed, and arguments are made in behalf of each one by different people. President Kennedy used a cluster of people in the PSAC pattern. President Nixon, I think, abolished the President's science advisor system. The present science advisor is, I believe, located outside the White House. Another distinguishing characteristic is the argument about whether or not there needs even to be a presidential science advisor. Several former Cabinet members who have spoken here have made an argument in favor of science advisors in each department. But the counterargument is how does that assist the President who is trying to evaluate scientific advice and data that he receives from an interested department on a problem?

At the time of the creation of the Miller Center, one of the hopes was that it could have some interdisciplinary outreach. Another reason the presidential science advisor topic has attracted us is that we thought of this as a topic in which inter-departmental and even inter-faculty cooperation is possible. Professor Robert Kretsinger of Biology, Dean Hugh Kelly of Physics and others have been unbelievably faithful in attending all our Forums on a wide range of topics. It has occurred to us that maybe we ought to find some topic where they would sit at the front table as the authorities on the subject and the rest of us would simply ask the relevant questions in drawing on them as sources.

In any event the subject of presidential science advisors is an area of genuine interest to the Miller Center. We thought it might be useful if Professor Greenwood would talk about this topic and then, as he sees fit, either use it as a point of departure or concentrate wholly on the issues raised by this subject. Ramifications are so numerous that maybe even if you wanted to, you couldn't limit it exclusively to the narrow subject of the President's science advisor. But both as a theorist and practitioner, Ted Greenwood has had a unique opportunity, unique at least among political scientists, to view the operations of this office and we are terribly pleased that he is with us today.

MR. GREENWOOD: Thank you. I thought I would restrict my remarks to the presidential science advisory process; perhaps that will stimulate a broader conversation.

The sources of information and advice to the President on science and technology or policies involving science and technology obviously are many. They include the departments and agencies of the government, all of which are bubbling proposals and analyses up to the Executive Office all the time. Among the relevant government agencies are several Executive Office units, including particularly the Office of Management and Budget, on a narrow set of issues the Council of Environmental Quality, and also the Office of Science and Technology Policy (OSTP). In addition, however, are all the Cabinet-level departments and many independent agencies whose missions and programs both affect and are influenced by science and technology. Other sources of information and advice include the media and individuals from many walks of life with whom the President may have contact. But if one wants to focus on the institutional presidency, then it seems to me that attention should be directed toward the Executive Office units and especially toward OSTP and the Office of Management and Budget.

What I would like to do is make some general remarks about OSTP, although OMB must necessarily be considered along the way. I will talk about OSTP's functions, the environment within which it operates and how it goes about doing its job.

Functions of OSTP

Let me begin by making a brief list of OSTP's functions. Some of these are given to the office by statute, the 1976 public law which created OSTP to replace its predecessor that President Nixon abolished. Other functions come directly from the President; still others just emerge out of the general environment. My list is not comprehensive, but it will be enough for the moment:

1. Providing advice to the President at his request in a wide variety of substantive areas having to do with science and technology; these days almost everything that the President deals with is included or could be defined to be. And I am really talking only about physical science and engineering here; if one included the social sciences, then really nothing would be excluded.

2. Commenting on proposals and ideas that come up from the agencies and providing advice and analysis to the President that both is independent of the agencies' sometimes parochial interests and takes the President's own perspective. This is one of the most important functions of the office.

3. Working with and helping other Executive Office agencies. These agencies are all staff to the President and they more or less cooperate in a competitive sort of way. Particularly important is helping the Office of Management and Budget craft the annual presidential budget. That actually is a statutory function for OSTP.

4. Interagency coordination, sometimes oversight and occasionally even management of certain policy areas, particularly those that involve several government agencies. All Executive Office units perform this function to some extent.

5. Recruitment and placement of personnel. This is an important function that attracts very little attention on the outside. The President's science advisor usually spends a good amount of time helping to locate and recruit people to positions all over the government in R&D management, regulation, and other areas where people with technical backgrounds are needed. These include, for example, the leadership of the National Science Foundation, the Geological Survey, all the other scientific organizations of the government, all the R&D components of the

agencies from the Defense Department to EPA, and many of the independent boards and commissions.

6. Helping resolve questions about how the government should be organized to deal with scientific and technical issues. Such organizational issues come up in every administration, although more in some than in others. OSTP participates in Executive Office discussions of such matters and often is consulted directly by departments and agencies as they reshuffle subordinate units, some of which always deal with science and technology.

7. Providing comfortable and knowledgeable entrée for outside members of the academic and industrial science and engineering communities to the President and others in the administration. This includes bringing policy papers to the attention of relevant officials, encouraging individuals to surface their suggestions and arranging occasional meetings with the President.

8. Other much less important functions include answering presidential mail, preparing talking points, and all the daily tasks that staff in the Executive Office or other government agencies have to spend time on.

Three Characteristics of OSTP's Environment

With this list of functions now before us, I would like to address three key characteristics of OSTP's environment that one must recognize and consider when evaluating OSTP as a part of the institutional presidency. I will list these first and then discuss each in turn.

First, there really is nothing that happens in the Executive Office of the President that could not happen without OSTP.

Second, OSTP does not own a presidential process.

Third, although OSTP is a very small unit, its mandate is truly enormous; this puts the office under great pressure.

OSTP is not Essential

The first point is that there is nothing that happens in the Executive Office structure that could not happen without OSTP. It is not an essential organization of the presidency. Other people or Executive Office units can perform its functions and at various times have done so. The government did not stop running when OSTP or, as it was called at the time, OST, was abolished by President Nixon. Let me say no more to justify this point but, taking it as given, explore its implications.

The argument for an OSTP cannot be that it is essential, that the wheels of governments would grind to a halt without it. Rather, the argument must be that in a society where science and technology are very important to so many of the things with which the President must deal, he and his staff can perform their jobs better if there is a White House staff office dedicated to the kinds of functions that I just enumerated. A separate, designated, tailored institutional body staffed with people with appropriate knowledge and experience can perform these functions better than they would be performed in the absence of such a body. Not that they otherwise would not be performed, but that they would be performed less well in the absence of a science advisor's office. They would be less systematically addressed and less well executed. That must be the thrust of the argument in favor of this kind of office. It has been persuasive to most Presidents since Eisenhower and certainly has been persuasive to the United States Congress, as exemplified by the act of 1976 creating a permanent OSTP.

OSTP Owns No Presidential Process

The second point, that OSTP owns no presidential process, requires greater explanation. If you look around the Executive Office, you soon discover that most other units do own a presidential process. The Office of Management and Budget, for example, owns the budget process. OMB runs it, manages it, and is in control of it. Everything that has to do with the budget—and that is almost everything the United States government does—comes through the budget process on an annual cycle and OMB is in charge. The Council of Environmental Quality sits on top of the environmental impact statement approval process and also the formulation of the annual presidential report on the environment. That is theirs: they write it or see to its writing. It gives them an automatic control over an admittedly narrow, but nonetheless significant, policy arena. The same thing is true of the Council of Economic Advisors. They are the primary source of the macro economic projection that the government uses to plan the future and they produce the annual economic statement of the President. The National Security Council staff, likewise, runs the process of interagency coordination of international and national security affairs. Although this process has varied somewhat from administration to administration, its basic structure and function has remained constant for at least twenty-five years, with the National Security Council staff in charge.

OSTP doesn't have such a process. Not that I would argue that it should, but the fact that it does not matters enormously for how the office functions within the Executive Office community. OSTP is highly dependent on how the President—each individual President—chooses to use it. This has varied quite a bit from one President to another. Differences have existed, for example, in what meetings the science advisor and his senior staff members have been invited to, how much access they have had to the President, how often the President has seemed to be turning to the science advisor and saying, "Dr. Keyworth," or "Dr. Press, what is your view on this question?" and how often the President has seemed to take the science advisor's advice when it is given. In the political environment of the White House, all of these things are noticed by everybody else and matter tremendously in the level of prestige and the level of authority that OSTP is able to command within the Executive Office structure. The power and influence of the office derives from the President and the extent to which others see OSTP as being close and important to him. There is no automatic source of influence.

In addition, the science advisor and his staff are highly dependent on others in the Executive Office for information and for access to the policy process. They need to get into the paper flow en route to the President and around the Executive Office circuit, to get access to budget documents and cables in the international field, and to attend an endless variety of meetings in order to know what is going on and to be part of it. But there is no automatic guarantee that any of this will happen. If one wants to close the science advisor out of a particular issue or render him generally ineffective (as happened, for example, long before Nixon finally abolished the position) all one needs to do is to cut off the paper flow and not invite him and his staff to meetings.

For the science advisor's office to be successful, his staff has to work very closely with those parts of the Executive Office that are guaranteed to be in the paper flow. The staff has to walk the halls of OMB, to be on friendly terms with the budget examiners, and to convince them that OSTP or the individual OSTP staff members themselves have something useful to offer. They have to do the same thing with the National Security Council staff and everybody else.

A relationship of mutual trust and helpfulness must be created if the OSTP staff is going to be effective. One of the ways that this has been facilitated in the past in the national security arena—it happened under Wiesner and under Press—is that a member of the OSTP staff has been jointly appointed between OSTP and the National Security Council staff. This arrangement had great advantages because it made OSTP into the science and technology arm of the NSC. Jobs were given to the particular individual through the NSC process and nobody really asked or cared very much whether he was working on a problem wearing his NSC hat or wearing his OSTP hat. Turf issues were defused and this gave OSTP easy access to issues and sometimes put the office in charge where it might otherwise have played a lesser role.

One result of this requirement for OSTP staff to work very closely and helpfully with other Executive Office agencies is that the independence of the office is constrained. To avoid getting closed out, OSTP staff have to be careful not to cross other people too often. They must use their limited political capital in a measured way. The last thing an OSTP staff person wants is to lose access to the corridors of OMB or other executive agencies with which they must work closely to be effective.

In a quite parallel way, OSTP staff must also develop good relations with sources of information in the departments and agencies of the government. To do this, a member of the staff must know—or learn pretty quickly—how the government works, within the limited set of agencies with which he or she tends to work. No one except the science advisor himself works with all agencies, but many staff members work with four or five or more. They have to know their way around, get acquainted with relevant individuals, and build alliances. If the science advisor's staff is not well enough plugged in to anticipate reasonably accurately for him what issues will come up in his discussions or meetings with senior administration officials and the President, and what positions everybody involved is likely to take, he cannot do his job effectively. Again, in order to maintain those kinds of relationships, OSTP staff members must give up some of their independence. Unlike OMB staff, who sometimes maintain quite adversarial relations with the agencies, OSTP staff simply cannot afford to operate that way. They would lose their friends, lose their sources of information, and lose their effectiveness.

A further result of this central point is that OSTP has no officially designated turf or ideology to protect. This is unusual for Executive Office units. OMB, for example, is the institutionalized advocate of restraint in government spending. The Council on Environmental Quality's (CEQ's) job is to advocate an environmentalist perspective. The Council of Economic Advisors (CEA) expounds the ideology of economic efficiency in both macroeconomist issues and regulatory debates. There is, therefore, a natural suspicion on the part of everybody in the government, and especially in the Executive Office, that OSTP is also an institutional advocate. The interest the office is naturally suspected of favoring is the nation's R&D community. Especially OMB, as the defender of the federal budget, suspects that OSTP wants to help the R&D community to get its hand into the federal till. Of course, to some extent, this suspicion is justified, resulting in a constant internal tension within the Executive Office. To be effective in its role as advisor to OMB on the R&D component of the federal budget, OSTP must be careful about how it makes its arguments and the extent to which it is perceived as representing the interests of its natural constituency.

The OSTP lost much of its credibility in the Johnson and Nixon administrations over this issue. The office came to be seen, maybe in part because it was closed out of other things, as an advocate of the R&D community.

Under Frank Press the office very consciously tried to avoid that reputation, while at the same time, actually acting the part. It was a very narrow line that Press tried to walk and he did it very cleverly. Early in the administration, he held a series of private discussions with the top officials of OMB. The result was a memo sent to all departments and agencies on the subject of basic research and development carrying the signature of the director of OMB as well as Press's. The memo encouraged agencies to be more forthcoming and more innovative in their budgets for basic scientific research. Support of basic science thereby became one of the main budgetary thrusts of the Carter administration and was so identified in successive Presidential budget messages. Although the basic research budgets did not go up in real terms as much as Press hoped, his intervention did bear significant fruit, and it was very cleverly done in the bureaucratic sense with OMB carrying much of the political burden.

OSTP is Small, But its Mandate is Large

Almost all issues are fair game for OSTP and there are rarely barriers preventing the office from getting into an issue if it wants to do so and can figure out how. But the staff is very small and has tended to be constrained by various personnel ceilings. Presidents tend to be concerned about the size of government and they are especially concerned about the size of their immediate entourage in the Executive Office. As a result, personnel ceilings get imposed. OSTP, like everybody else, has to work within those constraints.

OSTP can, however, within limits, circumvent such ceilings and augment its staff. It does this by borrowing people from other agencies. It can borrow a secretary from the National Science Foundation, a scientist from the National Institute of Health, an engineer from the Army Corp of Engineers, each one on detail for a year or two. This does not have to be done many times before the professional staff is perhaps fifty percent higher than it would otherwise be and the total staff is well over the ceiling. But since other agencies are paying the salaries, these additional personnel do not count against OSTP's allocations. As long as desks can be found, which is not always easy, borrowing people is a convenient way for OSTP to augment its staff. Without such augmentation, the office really could not function well at all.

In addition, of course, OSTP relies very heavily upon outside consultants, both formal and informal. I am not sure to what extent the practice has continued, but certainly in the Carter administration, OSTP had a large array of advisory committees focused on a wide variety of topics. This was a way of bringing outside people in and effectively augmenting the staff in significant ways. To illustrate how this can work, let me refer to how OSTP dealt with nuclear waste disposal, an issue with which I dealt extensively. At one point I was running a staff of six or seven people who were on loan from the Department of Energy, a national laboratory, the Geological Survey, the Nuclear Regulatory Commission and a university. They all more or less operated out of OSTP's offices for a period of five or six months writing policy papers. One thing about working in OSTP: when you ask for help, you usually get it. If you pick up the phone and call almost anybody in the country and say, "I'm calling from the President's Science Advisor's office and I want to talk to you about such and such," he or she will almost always talk to you about it. The staff does tend to use this ability to augment its own capability.

But even with the circumvention of ceilings the staff remains small; each individual must handle a wide variety of issues. No one has the luxury of dealing with only ten things at a time. Philip Smith, a former associate director of OSTP and my immediate boss while I was there, told me once that he looked for people who could get eighty percent of a problem right with fifty percent of the information and do it in two days.

Anyone who could not come close to meeting that standard could not function well at OSTP, or in any Executive Office unit. The entire structure works the same way. Decisions are made largely on intuition, with much less information and analytical underpinning than one would like. That is just the nature of the environment.

A further implication of the small size of OSTP and its large mandate is that it must try to pick and choose issues with care. The criteria must be not only that an issue has a major scientific or technological component and is important, but also that the office can actually make a difference; otherwise there is no point spending time. The management of scarce internal resources must be a matter of constant concern to the science advisor and his staff.

Finally, OSTP is by statute supposed to advise not only the President but also the Congress. The President's science advisor is to be available to testify before congressional committees on any subject they want. The 1976 statute specifies that he periodically send Congress formal reports. This responsibility to Congress adds a whole other dimension to the task of the office. In the Executive Office reorganization of 1977, Press managed to pass his responsibility for writing formal reports to the National Science Foundation. This made some of the congressional committee staff who drafted the 1976 statute irate, but Press rightly judged that the task of producing those reports would so consume his staff that they would be significantly impaired in performing their main duties within the executive branch structure.

This matter of the proper relationship of the President's science advisor to the Congress is a difficult one because if he (or anyone else in the Executive Office) is to be a trusted advisor of the President he must be guarded about what he says at congressional hearings or even to legislators in private. There is a long history of this at OST; indeed it goes back to the fifties. When the office was initially set up under James Killian, there was no requirement for the science advisor to talk to Congress and Congress was very unhappy about that. It was not until 1962, when President Kennedy created the Office of Science and Technology by the reorganization plan, that the science advisor was required to testify before Congress, and then only in his capacity as director of the new office, not as special assistant to the President. The science advisor then was still not confirmed by the Senate in those days. When Congress wrote the 1976 law, they made sure that the director of the Office of Science and Technology Policy would be confirmed by the Senate and that he would have to testify to the Senate.

In principle, of course, the President's special assistant for science and technology does not have to be the same person as the Director of the Office of Science and Technology Policy. One is a presidential office and the other is a congressionally mandated office. In practice, of course, they have been the same person and that is the only arrangement that makes sense. But the science advisor does wear these two hats and that does introduce a certain amount of tension into his role and the day-to-day operations of the office.

I would like to conclude by saying that I do think that this whole area of presidential science advice is a fruitful one for research. I think it is an area about which generalizations would be difficult to sustain empirically, in part because everything here, as in the rest of the Executive Office, is so highly dependent on personalities. But people who do research on the presidency must be used to that problem. Very little of the literature that I know on the subject of the presidential science advisor tries to integrate across different historical periods and make generalizations. Most of it tends to be either memoirs or former advisors or staffers reflecting on their own watch. It is an area where a broader historical sweep and some attempt to generalize are needed, and although that would be difficult, I think the effort would be well worth pursuing.

QUESTION: Let me ask a question about the role of the National Academy of Sciences. If you read the words, one of the major charges to the academy is to provide advice and information to various aspects of the government regarding science and technology. This is usually done by forming panels. They write reports and in the front of every report is an executive summary that one imagines that congressional aides read. I was just wondering, from your perspective, what role does the academy actually play? Are these reports read? Are they regarded as objective or are they simply regarded as advocacy statements for R&D? What role does all that play?

MR. GREENWOOD: That's a tough question. In fact, the academy itself doesn't even know the answer to that question. There is a little private operation now underway in the academy to try to think about the impact of its reports. In recent years that question has not been investigated systematically within the academy.

My own view is that there is considerable variation in the impact of academy reports. Some reports have a great deal of influence and others have none. The degree of influence depends on many things, not only the quality of the report but also whether the report falls on fertile ground. Most of the work the academy, or more correctly, the National Research Council, does is for the agencies and departments of the government under contract. Sometimes such contracts result from a congressional requirement written into law. There was one not long ago where Congress told the Food and Drug Administration to write a contract with the National Academy of Sciences to do a study on how the government should be organized to perform risk assessment. The FDA dutifully did so. Whether the FDA itself was really interested in that study and its results is not clear, but the Congress was.

Often studies go to the academy as a way of simply delaying action on an issue, putting it off. The agency thinks, "If we give the problem to the academy and tell them to study it for a couple of years, maybe it will just go away by the time the study is finished. In the meantime we can hold the wolves at bay by deferring to the on-going academy study." Sometimes jobs are really given to the academy because an agency wants help, either long-term help or sometimes, near-term help. I don't know how to generalize about the question of influence of NAS reports. I just do not have enough data.

In my own recent research on the regulatory process, I've actually looked in some detail at the interaction between the National Academy of Sciences and the Environmental Protection Agency in the risk assessments that the academy has done for the EPA. There have been standing contracts by which the Academy has done so many risk assessments per year. The decision as to which chemicals will be evaluated and what the schedule will be are made by EPA and NAS together. Some of the resultant reports became the basis for regulatory action. Some became the basis for deciding not to take regulatory action. Some of them just were put on a shelf and gathered dust. I haven't been able to figure out any systematic way of deciding ahead of time which is going to be which. Maybe there are ways of doing that, but a more thorough study than I have done would be necessary.

OSTP has not tended to use the academy very much. Press tried to on two or three occasions and found that the urgency of issues at OSTP tended to require different schedules than the academy was able to accomplish. Although Press got some promises out of the former President of the academy, Phil Handler, that things were going to be done and delivered quickly, they were not always lived up to. One of the things that Press, now as president of the National Academy of Science, is trying to do, is make the academy able to produce reports in a somewhat faster time frame. I do not know how successful he has been. I also have not noticed that Keyworth's been asking the academy for help, so maybe it has not mattered as far as OSTP is concerned. But the issue is important to other agencies too.

ADVICE ON SCIENCE
FOR THE U.S. GOVERNMENT

Norman Ramsey

NARRATOR: I am pleased to welcome you to a third Forum on the President and science advising. We may range a little more broadly today across the whole spectrum of government science advising. The Miller Center is interested in making some contribution in the area of the study of the President and his science advising system. The literature is relatively sparse. Most of you know the book by James Killian, *Sputnik, Scientists and Eisenhower,* which deals with the experience of the President's Science Advisory Committee following Sputnik. The controversy rages whether this was a unique period in American history when you needed not only a special assistant for the President on science but also an advisory committee. We have been discussing this whole area with the National Research Council and some of the people who participated in programs there, and Phil Smith recently sent us a copy of a report called, "The National Science Board and the Formulation of National Science Policy."

Professor Greenwood of MIT spoke on the subject recently, and we've had Frank Long and various others with whom we've talked. Not the least of the intellectual firepower as the Miller Center approaches the subject, obviously, are the very impressive and distinguished group of scientists at the University of Virginia, some of whom are with us this morning.

They need not be told, and perhaps none of you need be told, that Professor Norman Ramsey is professor of physics at Harvard University. He received his A.B. and Ph.D. from Columbia, and honorary degrees from such institutions as Cambridge, Case Western Reserve, Middlebury, and Oxford. He has served across the whole spectrum of science advising in the government and out as consultant, for instance, to the National Defense Research Committee; as expert consultant to the secretary of war; in the forties as associate division head of Los Alamos; and head of the Physics Department at Brookhaven National Lab. Following the Brookhaven period, I believe, he was professor and then Higgins Professor of Physics at Harvard; senior fellow in the Society of Fellows at Harvard; member of the Air Force Science Advisory Committee; scientific adviser to NATO; member of the Department of Defense panel on atomic energy; member of the executive committee of the Cambridge Electron Accelerator; member general advisory committee to the Atomic Energy Commission (AEC); a number of trusteeships in the science field; trustee of Rockefeller University, of the Carnegie Endowment of International Peace and of the Associated Universities, Inc. of Brookhaven Lab. Professor Norman Ramsey is the recipient of the Presidential Order of Merit for radar development work; he is the recipient of the E.L. Lawrence Award of the AEC; the Davisson-Germer Prize of the American Physical Society; the Columbia University Award for excellence in science and the Medal of Honor of the Institute of Electrical and Electronic Engineers. He has been president of the American Physics Society; is chairman of the board of governors, the American Institute of Physics; and has held numerous other honors. It seems to me we are indeed fortunate that this particular semester he is a visitor in the

Department of Physics at the University of Virginia, and we are delighted that as we begin to explore this subject that we can draw on his expertise.

PROFESSOR RAMSEY: Thanks very much. After hearing all my activities in that introduction I don't know how I have enough time left to do anything useful at all.

Need for Advice on Science

The first question I'd like to address is one for which the answer is fairly obvious, but the question is fundamental and should be discussed: is there a need for science advice in government? Clearly if there is no need for it one doesn't have to worry about how it's done; it can be eliminated. But the answer to the question is overwhelmingly positive and comes from several directions. One is that science and technology greatly affect the U.S. government in all sorts of ways. All one has to do is remind himself of the branches of government and in each one it is obvious that science is concerned. For example, they include problems of health, questions of safety, environmental problems, and productivity problems of inventions upon which the welfare of the country greatly depends. Agriculture is very deeply involved in scientific research. Defense is obviously particularly involved that way, and, on the opposite side, arms control is heavily impacted by science. For example, it now looks as if one can do rather better in detecting nuclear weapons tests than was thought possible not long ago.

But these are just examples. The entire area of government is affected by science and technology. Consequently, the government needs to do reasonably well in matters of science. Not only does science and technology greatly affect the government, but also, and inversely, the government greatly affects science and technology. Costs of research have now gone up in almost all fields to such an extent that everyone is greatly dependent upon rather large sources of support, and the only such source is the U.S. government. It's true that there is a considerable amount of applied research which is supported by industry, but then if one looks with care it is apparent that much industrial research is indirectly supported by the U.S. government through overhead charges or close association with government-supported research projects.

Finally, a key reason for needing science advice is that most government officials and legislators are not experienced in science themselves. The overwhelming majority of the members of Congress are lawyers.

The study of law does not give one much training in science. Even in the portions of government where there are quite a few scientists the scientists make up only a very small fraction of the total.

I found an illustration of this last week. I was meeting in Washington on some issue pertaining to science. One of the men who came to speak to us was an intelligent senator but very newly appointed to his position as chairman of the Subcommittee on Space, Science and Technology. For the U.S. Senate that's a task with major scientific responsibilities. The senator was frank to admit that one of his problems was that he'd never studied any science and had only been in the position about a year. The preceding year his assignment was on the Maritime Committee, which had little concern for problems of science and high technology. The fact that the senator recognized his limitations and even made a point of them was a good sign because he clearly needed to do so. But with this background he cannot on his own provide great scientific initiatives. He must then depend heavily upon science advice from the outside.

It is really very clear that there is a great need for the best possible science advice in government, for the sake of the government and the people and also for the sake of the scientists and scientific research.

Sources of Science Advice

What I would like to turn to next is how the science advising is done at present. There is a wide spectrum of ways by which science advising is done. It is fortunate on the whole that there is not a single unique channel which provides all of the advice. Such a monolithic structure is fine if all the advice is good but it is a disaster if the advice is bad. I shall divide the sources of scientific advice into several categories.

Unofficial Sources

The first category I'll talk about includes the unofficial channels of science advising, and I want to talk about that first for two reasons. In the first place it doesn't fit as well into a pattern as the official channels, and secondly it is important. Sometimes it's bad but nevertheless it is an important source.

The unofficial channels cover a wide spectrum and with marked differences of ways in which the science advice is given. One main way is through the general public—chiefly acting as individuals—writing letters to congressmen and writing letters to the President and government staff. Such letters do have an effect at times. The individual scientist visiting his own congressman is a valuable source of scientific advice. Many times a relationship between a scientist and a member of Congress is started by the scientist wanting to make sure that a particular bill is passed or rejected. Then suddenly the congressman finds that in his own district there is somebody who knows something about science. The member of Congress is having to vote on numerous science issues about which he knows little and is delighted to find there is somebody he can talk to. I think many good friendships have been formed in that way and many valuable bits of science information have come by that mechanism.

In general, my impression is that such advice is most effective when it's the individual scientist visiting his own congressman. In general, the chairmen of the committees are so harassed with all they have to do that they aren't very accessible. I think the local congressman is more interested in talking to a scientist in his district than the chairman of the committee is interested in talking to the world's most famous scientist because the chairman just doesn't have time for it and he has a feeling anybody who wants to talk to him is really lobbying for some measure or other and not to be fully trusted.

Other mechanisms that I would put in the unofficial category are the activities of individuals and ad hoc groups of individuals who do something technically good and relevant. An example is the current discussion of what is often called "nuclear winter"; namely, the atmospheric effects and the meteorological effects of a major nuclear war. There have always been some studies but most of them underestimated the magnitude of the problem. In the last couple of years there have been several individual groups of people in this country and abroad who have studied this problem and concluded it was a potential disaster. The study of this problem is now beginning to be taken over by the establishment. The National Research Council, which is a part of the National Academy of Science, is now undertaking a major study on the problem of nuclear winter. I think the general view so far is that this problem is a very serious concern which was not worried enough about at one time. The present reconsiderations have really started off as a result of individual groups just doing something on their own.

Another form of unofficial science advising is that by established groups. For example, the Council of the American Physical Society at intervals will pass resolutions when government actions are either wrong or missing. The government doesn't necessarily go the way the resolution says but the Physical Society is recognized as a responsible group and attention is paid to the recommendations of the society. In addition, the Physical Society at intervals undertakes specific studies pertaining to government and science, sometimes at their own initiative, sometimes at the request of the government. Several years ago when I was president of the organization the society started a study of solar voltaic cells. The question was whether the government should go into a big production crash program or should there be more research and development before going so far. I think the results of this study were quite useful.

Another example is a meeting I attended in Washington yesterday at the American Association for the Advancement of Science. On its own initiative, not at the request of the government, the AAAS has started a tradition beginning three or four years ago that as soon as the President's budget message is submitted, the AAAS has a committee that is all set to go with essentially a member from each of the major scientific societies. For example, Bob Park was there from the American Physical Society, and so on through the spectrum. The committee analyzes the President's budget on what its implications are and then publishes a book on the science implications of the budget. This book is not only of interest to scientists and the press; it is also of great value to Congress. It is a valuable independent analysis of the budget which comes out rather faster than most of the others. It is a book that stands on its own merits.

The final unofficial channel I'll discuss is influential individuals. Sometimes this influence is good, sometimes it's bad and sometimes it's disastrous—it depends on who the individual is. There are times when a President will have great confidence in a few chosen people and he may depend heavily on their advice. Such reliance is not unique to our system of government.

One of the clear examples was the relationship between Sir Winston Churchill and Lord Cherwell. The source of this relationship was their mutual respect which goes back to World War I when one of the main fears of pilots was the tailspin which was almost always fatal. Lord Cherwell as a physicist calculated what he thought was wrong and how one could get out of a tailspin by pointing the airplane down to pick up flying speed. Well, he concluded this theoretically and then tried to persuade some people to test it, but no one up to that time had ever been known to come out of a tailspin alive so he had trouble finding volunteers. Cherwell, being an amateur pilot himself, then tried it and acquired the distinction of being the first man in the world who ever deliberately went into a tailspin and the first man who ever survived a tailspin. This is obviously the kind of action that would appeal to Churchill and, as a result, in World War II Cherwell was a very influential personal adviser to Churchill. I think he had no official connection in any way but Churchill called on Cherwell for advice. That was all but it was highly effective.

In the U.S. at present, the President seems to pay particularly close attention to advice from Edward Teller. I am told that the big push for developing "star wars" defensive weapons technology came from Teller.

My net conclusion on individual advice from influential individuals is that it is of great importance; sometimes it is extremely valuable and good, sometimes it's terrible. It just depends on whether the advice is good or bad. I think there is no question but that this advising mechanism is here to stay. Such an influential individual can only be effective on a few major items, namely the items that can attract the attention of the President. In any organization, no person from the President on down can usually influence more than thirty or forty major items per year.

National Academy of Sciences

In discussing science advising, I am going from the less official to the more official sources. The National Academy of Sciences was established during the presidency of Abraham Lincoln for the purpose of giving advice to the government—both to the executive and Congress. Since World War II there has been a three-way split at the top; there is now the National Academy of Sciences, National Academy of Engineering, and the Institute of Medicine, and these three together cooperate quite closely. All three of them jointly sponsor the National Research Council which is usually the organization through which the various studies that they undertake are done. The academy and the National Research Council do hundreds of studies of technical problems of concern to the government.

The majority of studies are undertaken at the request of the government. But the academy is an independent body and starts many studies on its own initiative. The academy feels it is very important for it to be able to initiate studies.

These studies are often somewhat controversial. Many of the issues require study because of their difficulty so there is inevitable controversy about many of the recommendations. Frequently the academy recommendations are criticized.

One problem that is almost inevitable in anything like science advising is potential conflict of interest problems. If a committee has absolutely no conflict of interest in a subject it also may have no deep knowledge of the subject either. Conversely, a committee that's expert on the subject almost inevitably has some conflicts of interest. The academy tries very hard to overcome this problem as much as possible. The academy excludes from its committee people who have a very direct conflict of interest but includes people who are knowledgeable on the subject even though that means that they are going to have some interest in it and hence some potential conflict of interest. The academy does require that every committee member make clear what these potential conflicts are. The committee members have to prepare a written statement of the possible conflicts and they don't vote on particular issues that are directly related to their own interests.

Now a second thing the academy tries to do is have the committees balanced; that is, to have some members of the committee with a potential conflict of interest in one direction along with other members whose views are in the opposite direction. There may be criticism of a member of the committee who is clearly prejudiced but usually one finds another member of the committee who is prejudiced in the opposite direction.

Another criticism made of the National Academy committees is that they represent the scientific establishment, which in a certain sense they do. To compensate, the majority of the members of the committees that do the various studies are ordinarily not members of the National Academy.

The complaint by those who are members of the academy committees is that the committees are terribly time-consuming, which indeed they are. Criticisms are justified from all of these directions. Nevertheless, these studies under the National Research Council ordinarily provide good scientific evaluation of projects. Academy studies don't give immediate results. All their studies take six months or so, but for the kinds of things that really need a lot of looking into I think on the whole the academy studies do as well as anything else in providing carefully considered scientific advice to the government. Of course the advice isn't necessarily followed.

There are hundreds of academy committees and studies. There is a standing committee on road construction. There are National Bureau of

Standards evaluation panels and standing committees on a wide variety of subjects. In addition, there are a number of ad hoc committees appointed for special issues. For example, a committee was appointed to recommend what facilities should be pushed for the next decade in astronomy. Most of the recommendations of this committee are now being followed.

There is currently a study going on by the so-called Brinkman Committee to try to do the same thing for all of physics. There is considerable doubt that a committee can do as good a job in all of physics as the earlier astronomy committee had done simply because of the diversity of the subject of physics. It's not that easy to determine priorities in such a diverse subject. People's interests are so different. In astronomy everyone has somewhat similar objectives; in physics there are quite different objectives: some applied, some fundamental. For an academy committee to make priority judgments between quite diverse fields is probably unwise even though governments would like nothing better than a nice, clear priority list.

The academy committees are often involved in technical issues. I was chairman a couple of years ago of one such committee. There were claims that recorded acoustic evidence indicated there was a second assassin of President John Kennedy. Was the acoustic evidence valid? I ended up for some strange reason being chairman of what was called the Committee on Ballistic Acoustics evaluating that incident. We concluded that the evidence was not valid. But that is an example of a fairly limited technical issue. Actually it was a rather interesting project that came closer to a research project than most academy studies.

A study now going on that is of great importance is the one I referred to earlier on the atmospheric and meteorological effects of a really large-scale nuclear war.

In addition to the various committees that the academy appoints, whose participants are mostly not members of the academy, the academy has review panels which try to assure the quality of the committee reports. Every report of the academy is passed by a review panel which doesn't write the report and isn't really supposed to have too much influence on the report but nevertheless has to say that the report is a good one, that it was a reliable group that did the study and the conclusions followed reasonably from the work done.

National Science Board

Another advisory mechanism that is more directly part of the government is the National Science Board of the National Science Foundation which was established to give policy advice on science. It has been important in giving advice to the National Science Foundation as to how it should distribute its research funds. In principle, it also would be recommending national policies on science. I think it has so far been less influential in this direction than either the National Academy committees or the President's science adviser and the committees which he has established. Nevertheless, the National Science Board is an important advisory mechanism.

President's Science Adviser

The official source of science advising closest to the President is the President's science adviser and the committees he chairs. The most influential of these was the President's Science Advisory Committee which later became the White House Science Council. The man who is the President's science adviser actually holds a three-fold position: he is the President's science adviser in a personal capacity, he is chairman of the Science Council, and he is director of the Office of Science and Technology Policy, which is a totally in-government organization. All members of that office are government employees. This staff meets with those departments which have a fairly major scientific concern— agriculture, commerce, energy, defense, etc.—and together they try to coordinate activities.

The President's science adviser has both advantages and disadvantages over the previous advisory mechanisms that I've mentioned. Both the advantages and disadvantages arise from the same thing, being very close to the government. This is clearly an advantage in that the recommendations more frequently are adopted. A good example is the problem with which the Brinkman Committee is struggling in the National Academy. It is clear that sometime, somewhere along the line, even if one can't tell whether one kind of physics is better than another physics, somebody has to make an arbitrary decision on distribution of support. But it is dangerous to make such decisions until one is reasonably confident that the recommended actions will be approved. One does not want to turn one thing off in favor of another and then have neither of them be approved. Basically, the National Academy is in that awkward position. If it says we think A is better than B the committee can be quite confident that B isn't going to go forward but they have no confidence that A is going to go forward. In contrast, the President's science adviser can be much more confident than if he says A is better than B that A will be approved even if B is not. This means that he can do more.

On the other hand, there are disadvantages of being that close to the government: the President's science advisor is more restricted by government policies. He is not an independent person. He must, in that particular office, be at least reasonably compatible with the views of the President or he will cease to be effective. This limits what he can do.

We have had a President's science adviser for most of the years since World War II. The effectiveness of the office has oscillated up and down, the President's adviser sometimes being extremely effective. At its best the system has been very effective and has worked well. A good example is during the period of Eisenhower when Rabi and then Killian were science advisers. It worked extremely well and likewise between Kennedy and Wiesner. Although Kennedy was not President long, the relationship was extremely effective. Science advising hit its low point during the Nixon administration when basically the President's science adviser almost never saw the President. For much of his term, Nixon had a good science adviser but he was totally ineffective, and in fact the office gradually attenuated to nothing, and eventually was abandoned.

After the Watergate scandal came up, I decided maybe part of the reason was that the scientists were not very helpful in the problems of Watergate. At least if they had been I think they could have done a better job. Most scientists I know could have done various Watergate activities much more cleverly but they wouldn't have been very cooperative.

In any case, the President's science adviser was reinstated under the presidency of Gerald Ford. He appointed an extremely good man as science adviser, Guy Stever. I think Stever did a very good job of getting that science advising mechanism reestablished. He didn't have much time to put it into practice.

Our present science adviser is George Keyworth and he provides an interesting variation. Up to his appointment there was an effort made to try to pick a person who was a distinguished scientist as well as one that would be reasonably cooperative with the government. This time a deliberate effort was made not to pick a distinguished scientist but to pick somebody who would be a part of the government and would do more explaining government to scientists than the opposite direction. The man chosen for that was George Keyworth from Los Alamos. He has been quite effective. I don't always agree with the directions he wants to go in but nevertheless he has been effective in getting things done, much more so than many science advisers.

In the field of the physical sciences the budget problems have been favorably handled. In the biological sciences and medicine, it has been less so; and in social sciences, much less so, though not as badly now as a year or two ago when the new administration first came in. Keyworth is in a key position and he is getting things done. His priorities may be wrong but nevertheless he has been effective as far as getting his view across.

Advice to Government Departments

Science advice is not limited to the President's office but is also important in most departments. There are many departments that are concerned with science: HEW (Health, Education and Welfare) now HHS (Health and Human Services), Agriculture, Commerce, Defense, Energy, the Environmental Protection Agency, NASA, arms control—all depend tremendously on science. Most of them even have their own scientific advisory mechanisms, some on their own staff, but many have external advisory committees. Often these conflict. One committee will say something should be done by the Department of Commerce and another will say it should be done by the Department of Agriculture. So there is a problem of conflicting advice and sometimes the different committees mutually annihilate each other but that is not ordinarily true. When there are major conflicts it eventually is the task of the Office of Science and Technology Policy under the President to try to resolve them.

Advice to Congress

The final stage in any of the things that require legislation is of course Congress and again there is need for science advice. And from where does that come? One of the key places where it comes from is the executive branch, as most of the bills that are introduced by Congress come from the executive. Some scientific input has usually been obtained before the bills are presented but Congress usually wants to get its own independent advice. One of its sources is the General Accounting Office, which is a congressional agency, not part of the executive. The GAO advises not merely on accounting but on other topics as well when requested by Congress. The GAO studies often concern matters of science.

An Office of Technology Assessment in recent years has been established by Congress to provide advice on science and technology. Since the establishment of that office more science advice has come from that office than from GAO, but the GAO continues to play a role in matters that concern science.

Important sources of scientific advice are congressional aides. Each congressman and senator has a staff and sometimes one of the aides has some technical experience. This is a sufficiently valuable source of science input that in recent years many of the national scientific organizations have been providing so-called congressional fellows; namely, scientists who are interested in science and government who go and work initially for a year or so on the staff of one of the congressmen or on a congressional committee. A large number of them have turned out to be so valuable in that activity that they've eventually been hired by the congressmen or the committees they worked for to continue on their staff. This has provided a major upgrading of the scientific quality of the staffs.

The next major source is the hearings, and the hearings should be taken seriously. The hearings are valuable even when the congressional attendance is small. Often only one senator is there and he is probably out part of the time and passes the meeting off to a staff member. Nevertheless, even under such circumstances the hearing is a valuable source of learning for the committee members and staff and the written record helps a great deal.

Getting back to one of the items I mentioned earlier, individuals writing and seeing their own congressmen and senators have a very real effect. Particularly this is true in seeing if there is a congressman or senator in one's own district who happens to be on the committee that's relevant to the problem. A scientist in that area talking to his own congressman can be very, very helpful because the member of Congress usually feels badly in need of help and is glad to know there is somebody with interest and knowledge who comes from his own district.

Improvements to the Advisory System

Let me now take a few minutes to comment on potential improvements. The improvements that I can see aren't drastic changes. Most of them are just following the present procedures but doing them better. For example, it's quite clear that the best possible President and the best possible Congress should be elected. Science advice at its very best can only make an excellent President do better and prevent a bad President from doing worse, and that's about as far as it can go. One reason a good President is much more effective is his ability to recognize when he is getting good advice.

Another thing which is needed is better science education for the nonscientists. The ones who go into government should have better knowledge of science. There is just a tremendous amount of interaction between science and government and most government officials need to be somewhat knowledgeable about science. A person with no knowledge of science but who is receiving advice on science issues confronts two opposite dangers. One is that he may totally ignore the advice because he doesn't understand it. The other danger, which is equally serious, is that he may be so impressed and overwhelmed that he swallows it hook, line and sinker without evaluating what's good about it and what's poor about it. Likewise, he may fail to distinguish between advice and advisors that are good and those that are bad.

Most science concentrators in college have a feeling that their education has been awfully narrow if they haven't taken anything beyond the minimum number of required nonscience courses. Most of them will take quite a few beyond the minimum. On the other hand a large fraction of the nonscience students reluctantly take their one required science course in the science that has the reputation of being the easiest one, whether it's relevant or not, and feel that that's sufficient. And that's too bad. Maybe we should make the courses more interesting, I don't know. But something should be done to provide better science background for more people in government.

There also needs to be a greater willingness for scientists to participate in government operations. Such participation has its problems. If a professor of government is asked to spend four years in Washington, he's probably a better professor of government when he returns to his university for all the government experience he's had. On the other hand, a research scientist asked to spend four years in Washington is away from the forefront of his field for that time. When he comes back to his home institution he's worse off for the experience rather than better off unless he wants to go permanently into science and government policy. So such participation is a real sacrifice; nevertheless it is important for it to occur. We need more people who are willing and able to do so.

My final comment on improvements is a warning in the opposite direction; namely, we want to avoid making changes that make matters worse. Often we say we are going to improve something so we change it but we should remember that it is easy to make matters worse. The present procedure is rather cumbersome and it certainly could use some streamlining. On the other hand, in some respects it is remarkably effective and certainly more effective than it once was. On the average it works. For example, many people think that all of science should be concentrated in one department, a Department of Science, so there would not be science in the other departments. It's quite clear that the diversity of the departments needing science is much too great for this concentration to be desirable. Agriculture is clearly going to want to have its own science activities. And it's quite different from the kind of science activities that are needed at the Bureau of Standards.

Another dangerous change currently advocated by some is to put in various restrictions on the free exchange of scientific information. One way is by inventing a new category of classification which is known as "unclassified but militarily sensitive." If information is very sensitive it ought to be classified. I'm a believer in security when it is really needed but it must not be allowed to creep into areas where it does more harm than good.

A second harmful means of restricting information exchange has been the use of export controls on information. There is export control now of information. The following experience happened to the president of the American Vacuum Society and the president of the Optical Society when they had an open meeting—a regular scientific meeting. They began receiving threats from government officials. They were told they had to exclude all foreigners from the meeting because papers at that meeting would be exporting information if there were any foreigners there. These were open scientific meetings where as a matter of principle there is no attendance check. The presidents of the societies were threatened with jail sentences. Nothing ever happened but nevertheless it was not very comfortable for them and the threatening phone calls were means of intimidation. The whole success of U.S. science has largely been due to the free interchange of information. That's where ideas are generated. Destroying this free interchange will greatly impede scientific progress.

Another suggestion on the operation of science is to avoid excessive regulation. Government micro-management of research can sometimes be an attractive thing for the government but it usually impedes scientific progress.

It would be helpful in scientific research projects if one could avoid drastic budget fluctuations. For example, when the Reagan administration first came in they decided that all of the educational expenditures in science were really a total waste. The education budgets were drastically reduced. The social science budgets were almost eliminated. Two years later or so the government decided these were rather important after all. The education budget is coming back up and the social science budget is at least not being further diminished. But it would be best to avoid these drastic fluctuations.

These are my own views on advice on science for the U.S. government. I would welcome questions, corrections, comments and suggestions from all of you. I recognize that many of you gathered here have had much experience in both government and science.

NARRATOR: If we were at Monticello we'd probably say that never has there been more scientific imagination around this table since Jefferson sat at the table alone. It certainly ought not to overawe those of you who are not professors of physics or chemistry. We hope you will raise questions, too. I thought as you mentioned unofficial contributions, someone in this room was quoted at great length in today's press on the health conditions and dangers of contaminated wells in rural areas. Mrs. Treva Cromwell has been an authority on the subject for twenty years.

PROFESSOR RAMSEY: This is important. Even though such work doesn't seem to get an immediate response, it does eventually. It takes a long time sometimes. The process should be speeded.

QUESTION: You mentioned the desirability of members of Congress and others in the government having some scientific background and I wish in a way that you had emphasized it more because it seems to me that this is basic to a lot of the problems of passing on the scientific method. And if you will pardon me just one second I'll give you an example as to what I mean.

Several years ago I ran into a senator friend of mine in the National Airport in Washington and we argued for quite a long time, saying that a particular drug was the most wonderful thing for cancer and he had introduced legislation in Congress to promote it. He got the idea from one individual. He is trained as an economist and I don't think he had any concept of the scientific method. I think every lawyer and every legislator should have some training in the scientific method and I hope you agree with me.

PROFESSOR RAMSEY: Yes, I fully agree with you.

QUESTION: As a science educator, among other things, I'd like to address this question. I think the present structure of the universities does not permit the teaching of science to nonscientists. The physics department and other departments have tried in the past to introduce courses of that nature. The problem is the structure. The one I introduced, for example, was aimed at people from the graduate business school and the law school. I got a fair number of students who at some sacrifice came to the class and I guess they learned something from it. It may not have been the most ideally structured course that one could imagine but I think they got something out of it. But in general these things are not encouraged and the structure of full-time equivalents and things of that sort don't permit small seminars very easily. And of course the law schools themselves and I suppose the graduate schools of business are so focused on their own methods courses that they don't like to see their students taking many outside courses. They certainly don't encourage it. So the present structure of our educational system is against it.

One would like to require them to take more science but I don't think your average student who is headed toward a career in law or business truly appreciates the value of it. They tend to be practical people and they don't really appreciate the value of it until they've run into a need for it, let's say, because they're taking a course in dangerous products legislation or something of that sort. I used to participate in teaching something like that in the law school. That was when people started to see the value of it, but as freshmen, sophomores in the undergraduate school, they don't really see the value of it. They see that it is something to be endured and gotten through because all their contemporaries see it as something to be endured and gotten through. The people who do it, do it because they like it.

PROFESSOR RAMSEY: I think that's right. I agree with your point on the structure but I think it's also the general point of view. I think somehow or other most scientists have gotten convinced somewhere along the line when they are undergraduates that if they are ignorant of everything except science they are somehow being too narrow, that it really isn't the right thing. Most of them would have that feeling. They have a slight inferiority complex if they pay no attention to politics. In contrast, it's just the opposite with many of the people who are not going into science. They take the minimum requirement but don't intend to do anything beyond that.

I think the structure and the attitude work together, and this is partly the reason the structure is the way it is. I think most scientists, though they are not experts on politics, at least know something about it, at least read the newspapers. The vast majority of nonscientists don't do the same thing. However, some do; there are some who subscribe to, say, *Scientific American.* There are excellent ways in which one can keep up; *Scientific American* is indeed one. This is at a fairly high level. There are other lower-level things one can read. The fact that some nonscientists are interested in science is evidenced by *Science 84* which was recently introduced for popular consumption. It has been a great success. There are a large number of subscribers.

QUESTION: I'm in health. We're going at it in a different way. We think the administrative assistants run the government without any question. We did a survey about three years ago and only two percent of administrative assistants on the Health Committee in the House or Senate knew anything about health. So we are going to bring them down here to the Health Center.

PROFESSOR RAMSEY: You mean have them get a leave?

QUESTION: Two weeks, three weeks.

PROFESSOR RAMSEY: That's very good. I think that is an excellent thing.

QUESTION: We will at least let them know this part of health. That's one statement.

The other statement is you forgot women in Washington. You forgot Margaret Mahoney and all those people.

PROFESSOR RAMSEY: I believe I used the word scientist, which includes males and females. There are key women. There are some very key women in all of the levels, but not as many as there should be. In the physical sciences there is a great problem; we just don't have enough of them in the field at all, particularly in physics. The number we can call on is very small.

QUESTION: The question I'd really like to ask you is to go back to the model from World War II, one in your area and one in health. When we lost quinine we had to find a substitute and as you know Jim Shannon had the malaria project at Columbia. But that wasn't really at Columbia; it was all over the country.

PROFESSOR RAMSEY: I think Bob Woodward was working on that.

QUESTION: And many experts came together for a specific purpose. Now I think Merrill Ture did the same project in your area. We don't have that now. Having sat in on a lot of study sections in the House, I see there is a lot of waste of money. I realize my friends in academia will shoot me, but is there a time when we've got to worry less about individuality than what the problem is, and if there is such a time, how do you see it done?

PROFESSOR RAMSEY: I agree with you that there is some waste. But scientists do come together for cooperative projects when that is best. Quite reasonably it occurs first and most intensively in the places where the cost of the research is most expensive because those are the places where it is needed most.

Take, for example, the field of particle physics—high energy physics. This requires huge accelerators. Actually the first recommendation for consolidation came from a committee of which I was chairman of in 1963. It was a joint committee established both by the President's Science Advisory Committee and by the General Advisory Committee of the Atomic Energy Commission and this committee was to make a recommendation on what should be done for accelerators in the future. There were proposals for twenty-five different accelerators that different universities wanted to build, costing a huge sum of money and also not being all that much more interesting than the biggest accelerator that existed. Our committee reached the firm conclusion that we should build none of those, but what we should do is pick only very major steps toward high energy and approve only these steps. This recommendation was unpopular at first with those whose projects were rejected but eventually almost everyone agreed this was the right thing to do. At

Fermi Lab we built a single very high energy machine for use by scientists throughout the world.

This occurred first in the expensive field of high energy physics and, depending on how budgets go, this is going to occur in other fields as well. Now there are also disadvantages to doing such cooperative projects; one is stuck with program advisory committees to select for approval only a few of the proposed experiments. I know it is very discouraging when one's promising experiment is rejected. But the committees are forced to do it. I think the U.S. should not force such consolidation until it is really necessary. But it is a way in which one can do things more economically and I know that other fields have also been doing such consolidation a bit more. It is happening, for example, at the National Magnet Laboratory at MIT, where for experiments requiring really high field magnets, it's better to go to the Magnet Lab for the experiment than to try to build up one's own facility for temporary use in Virginia.

QUESTION: I've always been intrigued at the studies of government executives of how they organize their own staffs. I refer often to Robert Lovett; he wanted to have at least two assistants and preferably a lawyer and a scientist because if they were trained fully and knew how to recognize facts and face up to unpleasant things and had the courage to do it, they could help the man they were assisting in government. He emphasized the need to have staff people around who could recognize unpleasant facts of life when you ran up against them. And I think every scientist at the top level is a good deal like a judge. Judges are supposed to be impartial. I think it was either Holmes or Cardoza who said every scientist has his own inarticulate premise and this is the thing that often guides his judgment, sometimes to his benefit, sometimes to disaster perhaps, in terms of making wise decisions.

PROFESSOR RAMSEY: I think perhaps scientists do operate a little bit differently than lawyers, especially pertaining to a hearing. Basically a hearing is considered to be fair if each side has a chance to present its case. That's not really what a scientist will do. You can get a group of them together, they may have their initial prejudices but as they study the problem they may go in the opposite direction to that from which they started. They are not advocating one side even though they may have their initial prejudices. They are primarily seeking the truth.

NARRATOR: May I ask a question from the empty chair? The empty chair might have been occupied by some of the people we consulted when we asked should the Miller Center look at this subject. Isn't it important that the President organize his science advising in a way that helps him do the best job on making decisions? And two or three ex-Cabinet people we talked to said there is a real danger in that. They argued the President's Science Advisory Committee (PSAC) became in effect a pressure group, a lobbying group, for all kinds of financial support to science. And their argument was it was better therefore to locate scientists in the departments and have them advise within specific areas. Is there any merit at all to that criticism?

PROFESSOR RAMSEY: Well, I think there is probably merit to that kind of criticism on any activity in or out of science. There are science activities concentrated in departments, but there is a clear need for something more central. I personally think there is a very great value served by a central organization. Different departments each will want to do certain things. The Defense Department by itself would happily spend all the science money on its own science. You have to have the others, too, and you have to have some place at which the work can be coordinated and where some of the hard decisions can be made. I would say PSAC, though it only recommends, very frequently recommended reductions. That's true, they obviously did what they thought was best so that they may include more things. But actually they very frequently have recommended against doing things because of cost and things of that order.

NARRATOR: What do you do if the President doesn't care to talk to scientists? The Killian book makes it clear that Eisenhower enjoyed talking to scientists. He referred to "my scientists" and he even described what the scientists wanted to do. But some Presidents seem to be nervous about having to talk to them.

PROFESSOR RAMSEY: Well, my impression is that in the Nixon regime, the President went to the opposite extreme. He was more than nervous about talking; he just wasn't interested at all. There was no communication then and there is deep trouble when that occurs. We are still paying the penalty of that period at the present time. Many things fell quite far behind at that time and it's not easy to catch up. This is true both in the support of science and many other things.

QUESTION: I just want to underscore the point that you were making because I was in the Ford White House. We were looking past November. They did not expect the OSTP to last or that it would be carried over for just the reason you're saying. The presumption was that it would become a spokesman for outside interests and the Executive Office of the President doesn't want that, a problem that the Council of Environmental Quality never overcame. It was not consequential in any administration, whether it was the Nixon or Carter one.

QUESTION: A quick question. Why is the President or the executive branch hostile to spokesmen from outside interests? I should think they would welcome input from outside interests.

QUESTION: When advisers become public or become looked upon by the public as their advocate to the President, the President doesn't like it. You can't picture OMB coming out with the position that is contrary to what the administration policy is.

Now you might say we have an example in the Council of Economic Advisers at the moment but that is certainly not the customary role of the Council of Economic Advisers.

PROFESSOR RAMSEY: I think it is indeed true. The President's science adviser in any administration is restricted. Maybe he shouldn't be making public attacks on the presidency, and maybe he should get out if he feels sufficiently opposed. But on the other hand, he is representing a different view, and the President needs to get some different views represented to him. My impression is that the OMB view is also a prejudiced view. I think everybody has a prejudiced view somewhat. Everyone approaches an issue from one position or another and my impression is that on the average the advice that usually comes from the President's science adviser and particularly through OSTP, being really a government group, has predominantly been for what is good overall, not just because it's good for science. But even so it may appear to a person who doesn't want to spend any money on a science that that's a bad thing.

QUESTION: Well, it may be either a nonproblem or a problem without a solution, but I've had the impression on some occasions in the past that the science advisory system does not really represent the social sciences or may in fact be hostile to the social sciences. Is there any cure to that?

PROFESSOR RAMSEY: Well, in the first place, originally it wasn't set up for the social sciences. But on the average it has been more helpful than most parts of the government to the social sciences. For example, with the drastic cuts that occurred in the beginning of the Reagan administration, the social sciences were wiped out almost completely. Actually at that stage, the various science boards, national science boards, the vast majority being in the natural sciences, came out quite strongly that they wanted more support of the social sciences. So I would say no, they have not been hostile, but they've not really felt it was their primary business. The fact is that clarification on this could probably be good in the sense that there is always a little lack of clarity when one uses the phrase "the President's science advisers." Does that mean advisers representing all science, science including social sciences, or is it just the natural sciences? I think because of this lack of clarity, social science may sometimes be neglected. On the other hand it's not necessarily true that they would want to have the same person as their science adviser. Maybe there should be a social science adviser.

NARRATOR: I'm sure I speak for all of you in thanking Professor Ramsey for taking time to come over to this building when he's very active, I gather, in another building on the grounds. I would hope that this inquiry, plus one or two others that we've had, might lead the Miller Center in the direction of studying this problem in greater depth.

PROFESSOR RAMSEY: A lot could be done on this problem.

THE PRESIDENT'S SCIENCE ADVISING

David Billington

NARRATOR: Before I introduce Professor Billington, let me mention how we began our discussions on the President and science advising.

The Miller Center is the only center in the country that exclusively concentrates on the study of the American presidency. That, in part, was an act of judgment by the University officials, but it also was influenced by the wishes of the donor who made possible the establishment of the Center.

Mr. Miller was a graduate of the Law School. He observed that there were public affair centers elsewhere, including Princeton obviously, your school, but he thought there ought to be a major center in the South if possible. So he visited some southern universities and colleges, made and asked for proposals, and got reactions. The end of the story is that, fortunately, the University of Virginia received his donation. The Center was established in 1975. Most of us who work at the Center now have been here essentially for seven years. That has been the more active period in its history. We have scholars in residence; we have younger scholars who are pursuing their degrees; we hold forums about once a week except in the cold snowy weather. In January we stay away from these things but we do try to have some kind of formal or informal discussion.

Usually these forums are part faculty, part community, attended by thirty or forty people. The subjects of the forums have been particular presidencies. We have published portrait volumes on Roosevelt, Truman and Eisenhower. We are finishing a volume on Kennedy and starting a volume on Nixon. They deal with the problems of the presidency, the nature of the presidency, themes of that kind.

We are continually asking those with whom we meet, "What are the unexplored areas of the presidency?" One that surfaced very early was the whole area of science advising in the presidency. Every President has done it a little differently, as you know. Eisenhower apparently liked to have very strong and forceful people around him with different points of view. He consulted Teller but he also had Kistiakowsky and Rabi and people of that kind. Kennedy had a large group around him. Nixon abolished the use of a science adviser in the White House. We have been told this is such a vital area because what the President is told about scientific topics determines his views about Star Wars, about the environment, about all these policy issues that keep coming up. Half a dozen public officials who came here have said that in their service as adviser to the President they simply were unable to grasp the scientific intricacies of certain issues. Several of them have said the only thing that the President can do is to pick his scientists and hope that from a given scientist he will get the soundest possible advice. Other people have said that science advising ought to go on at the level of the departments. To place it at the White House level just continues the trend that already exists of exporting everything out of the departments into the White House.

I gather you have the feeling that science has a better chance of contributing if it's outside the government free and independent. Somebody quoted you to that effect. Maybe that's a misquote. But in any case we welcome a wide range of thinking about the problem.

David Billington, as you all know, is professor of Civil Engineering in the School of Engineering at Princeton. He is the Phi Beta Kappa lecturer at the university this year. When we heard he was coming, we invited him to speak on this subject.

MR. BILLINGTON: Well, the idea of science advising to the President is not something which I have knowingly ever commented on before. I am wondering where the quote came from. But I do have some ideas about government policy and science and technology. You did not use the word technology, but I am an engineer so of course I tend to see things somewhat differently.

As I understand it, what the President really needs advice on is technology, not science. I mean the President does not much care about quantum theory, relativity theory or cloud chambers. What he cares about is what is going to work, what is going to be built, and the impact of those things both politically and environmentally. So I think I would change the terms of the discussion from the way it is normally discussed. I really do not think that Presidents need a science adviser; what they need is a technology adviser.

Of course, some scientists are so knowledgeable in technology that they could fill the bill so I do not mean to rule them out just because of their titles. But I really do think that there is a fundamental difference between science and technology. The two terms are linked together very often as if they are the same sort of thing.

So let me be specific now and make the distinction that I see between natural science and engineering. The scientist is concerned obviously with discovering natural things, things that have always existed, and with understanding these things. The scientist often works in a controlled laboratory setting or in some office and is seeking generality of theory. That's the goal of science.

The engineers, by contrast, are not interested in discovery but interested in design, making something that works. They are not interested in the natural world but interested in the artificial world, the world created by people. They are not interested in what has always been there but interested in what has never been there before. They are not interested in controlled, laboratory study but interested in the full-scale observation of working objects. The crowning achievement for the engineer is what works in the field, not what can be discerned from pieces in a laboratory. And, finally, generality of theory has essentially no meaning for engineers. They are interested in specificity and practice. From the point of public policy, many scientific things have almost no meaning to the general public. The public does not care about all those things.

Now of course in a kind of a mythological way they do. I mean they always cared about Einstein's great ideas when they were confirmed. They became a kind of a public mythology and Einstein was held up. The general public had no idea what his work meant. But it became the kind of mystique of science as an elevated activity, which indeed it is.

Now there is of course some connection between science and engineering, no doubt about it. Scientists during the war, for example, were able to do lots of first-rate engineering. There was much interconnection, and there still is a lot of interconnection. But, nevertheless, I want to establish that important set of distinctions.

Now, what is engineering or technology? I use the two terms synonymously; society's problems with technology are in fact the problems of modern engineering. There is a broader use of the term technology which carries us back to Greek technology and Mesopotamia. But they are not the problems that worry us today.

The problems that arise today are the ones that have come up since the industrial revolution and they involve what we define as modern engineering. Now what are they? I say there are two sides to modern engineering. On one side are the structures, the fixed objects. On the other side are the moving objects—the machines. And these have quite different characteristics. The structures are static. They are built locally, they are custommade. They are essentially public works—fot instance the bridge. Machines are dynamic. They are global. They are made to be used anywhere. They are mass-produced and they are essentially made by private industry. So when talking about technology you have to make that distinction. What you try to apply to the Ford Motor Company will simply not apply to the Corps of Engineers.

You remember the famous case of George Romney who had been head of American Motors. He came into the government as head of the Department of Housing and Urban Development (HUD) and his objective was to mechanize building. He was going to turn the construction industry into an automobile-type industry and of course it was a colossal failure. Not only did he waste a lot of money but there was very little that came out of it because of this fundamental confusion. So you have to separate these two things.

The next idea really is to understand modern engineering. In addition to those individual objects—the bridge and the automobile—there are big systems of engineering. The highway network is a system of engineering and the water treatment plant is a process of engineering. The process is a system in which things change whereas the network is a system in which things do not change.

If I were to make a slightly more refined definition of engineering, I would say it has four ideas associated with it: there are the structures and the machines, then there are networks and processes. These correspond roughly to the four major divisions within engineering; structure corresponds to civil engineering; the machine to mechanical engineering; the network to electrical engineering; and the process to chemical engineering. Now all of them are mixed in the real world. I am just making a model, as we always do in academic life. But I think it is very important from the point of view of how these affect the public.

Because structures are public works—their owners are local governments and the relationship between the public and the objects, or the public and the profession, is always directly in the local political environment.

Machines, on the other hand, are by and large not made by government; they are made privately in private industry. So that whereas the government *owns* the structures, the government *regulates* machines.

When you come to the systems you get to much more complicated questions. The networks might be characterized as public utilities. You have the railroads, power supply, communication networks, water supply. They are networks of technology that involve structures and machines. They always involve an interplay between public and private, but the government is always heavily involved. You think of Amtrak for railroads, TVA for power or water regulation, AT&T for communications. Think of the Imperial Valley in California, the making of the whole state of California. That is a system, a network really, of water.

Whereas when you come to the fourth characteristic, the processes, you think largely not of public utilities but of private industry. But you also think of the public environment when you think of these processes. You think of chemicals, fuels, air and water quality which are aspects of the processes associated with big industries.

This scheme seems to be important. But I really believe that there is a basic confusion that arises from not recognizing these kinds of differences.

QUESTION: Back to your first point where you made the distinction between science and technology. Correct me if I am wrong, but I understand that you would, from a public policy point of view, say that technology or engineering is more important than science.

MR. BILLINGTON: Absolutely.

QUESTION: Then what role should the government have in basic scientific research? One argument is that technology will take care of itself because of the profit motive. The best example that comes up is DNA and what all that has brought forth. Yet the basic research is the part that the government should focus on. That is where the grant money should go because that is where the long-term payoff comes in.

MR. BILLINGTON: Historically, that is not true. Yet this view was propagated with the founding of the National Science Foundation and a report written by Vannevar Bush. He started out by saying that all technology has sprung from basic research. Well, it is wrong. A group of scholars has been probing that question which is obviously a very important question. If you are arguing that technology has sprung from science you must be able to show that. Yet you cannot show it. Let me give you an ad hoc example. When Carnot began to describe his theory of thermodynamics, what is the first chapter devoted to? It is devoted to a discussion of James Watt and the steam engine. In other words, science there was applied technology. It comes directly out of the technology. Without the steam engine there would have been no thermodynamics. So right from the start, from the industrial revolution, you find that that model basic-research does not hold up. Now the world is always more complicated than the academic mind wants to make it, so even what I am saying is not completely correct. But I still think that what Vannevar Bush was doing is definitely off-center. Bush himself was an engineer, but because of the terrific prestige of science he was making a case which would appeal politically at the time. In order to get the National Science Foundation founded in a country which has always been noted for its pragmatism, its emphasis on technology, he had to make the case for the primacy of science.

There have been a series of studies trying to trace technological innovations since World War II back to basic science. They cannot do it. There are two different studies that came to radically different conclusions. One of the studies was more or less unbiased but the other was by the National Science Foundation which naturally had to show the importance of basic science. So the history of technology, which is a relatively new field which began formally about 1958, was really in a way stimulated by this argument. And for the last thirty years these issues have been discussed. By now I would say it is a mature field.

In 1976 when they published the symposium volume on the relationship between science and technology, there was not a single scholar who was willing to defend the Bush position, not a single one. They said, "That is beyond debate now, that is just wrong." The basic agreement was that these were two independent fields—that new science builds on old science, new technology builds on old technology. Certainly scientific research is very important. I am not speaking against scientific research at all. Fundamental to the human being is the curiosity of finding out what is there, and it does from time to time have application. But in the long run it is not the best way to get applications. It should be justified on other grounds which I think are more fundamental.

QUESTION: What about the freedom argument? One reason foundations and government ought to support basic scientific research is that people have to be free to pursue their research wherever the evidence leads them. The "usefulness of useless science" idea is that you do useless research that you know is unlikely to lead to a breakthrough in any applied area. Nevertheless, it is likely to open up unexpected areas. The scientists at the Rockefeller Foundation always defended support for that kind of research since that is the kind of research that corporations and business concerns would never support. Is any more freedom needed for basic science research than industry technology? Are technology people just as free to pursue undirected research?

MR. BILLINGTON: Undirected research has had little meaning to technology. Our greatest works of technology are highly directed. They are disciplined by the need to make something that works. That is the goal. It is not to find out about things, it is to make something that works. Now when you want to make something that works you are led into all kinds of very deep problems. The people who tried to make steam engines were led into very deep problems and out of that came thermodynamics. So it does not mean that you do not learn to understand the deepest mysteries of life from directed research.

Another mistake is equating technology with private industry. I have been very insistent that that is only half the argument. Public works are not private industry. The creation of the road, bridge, all those networks, all those immense things, have a quite different motive behind them than does private industry. People could argue that the Bell Labs, which is private industry, is the most creative technological environment in the world. But I put that in the middle category because that is a regulated public utility. It is certainly under the profit motive and you cannot argue that that does not produce some great things. General Electric is the same way, the great General Electric lab.

QUESTION: Would you consider Bell Lab scientific or almost purely technology?

MR. BILLINGTON: Well, that is very difficult to say. If you ask them they will say scientific. If you ask the Board of Directors they might say technological. I think the creativity has come about because of the profit motive. They allow their people terrific freedom but they also have a mission. The development of the transistor was a mission-oriented, technological achievement. They discovered all kinds of things which we would call science, but at the same time it was mission-directed and that is why it was so fruitful.

QUESTION: It is always a surprise to me that the scientists I've talked to have reacted sort of negatively to the Star Wars proposal. They say it is just an utter impossibility—it's just dreaming. What has always struck me is that scientists, instead of getting excited about trying to come up with the technology and match the purpose, have almost universally just panned this whole idea. Why would they be so negative? I mean here is something that needs to be done, here's the money for it.

MR. BILLINGTON: I mean the scientist is not trying to discover how to make something go up there, that is the technologist who is trying to do that. The technologists are often excited about such things. But the scientists are often not. On the other hand, some engineers have criticized the Star Wars promise.

QUESTION: Would agricultural research—trying to make hybrids to increase production—be under science or technology? That is clearly purpose-oriented but that is also pure science I would think. It is all test-tube work done through germinating and crossing different kinds of seeds.

MR. BILLINGTON: I agree with you it is a complicated thing. I think that if you talk about food production in the sense of the Imperial Valley that I mentioned, that is very clearly a technological thing. In the treatment of water you could say there is a lot of chemistry; there are a lot of test tubes. If you go into a laboratory of environmental engineers, there are a lot of test tubes there. Certainly there is a lot of chemistry and biology that goes into it but nobody doubts that they are doing engineering. The research part of it is a very small part because everything depends upon if it works in the field. Now I am not sure about agriculture. I just do not know enough about it really to comment intelligently. But I suspect that the small amount of research that is done in the laboratory, which may look scientific or may look like natural science research, is really not that at all. The difference between chemistry and say chemical engineering is that the latter builds something full scale that produces. The engineer is worried about so many different things that a scientist never even thinks about. But most of what comes out of chemical research is not even applicable. I do not mean to imply that undirected research does not sometimes have utilitarian value. It certainly does, there is doubt about that.

A very interesting study was done of the British chemistry fraternity. It turned out there were two different fraternities: there were academic chemists and the industrial chemists. The industrial chemist was somewhat like the chemical engineer and the academic chemist was really a kind of a brother to the academic physicist. The academics were winning Nobel Prizes, and these others were maybe getting patents for things. They were really in different worlds. And I think that is important to realize. The chemists in a big industry have to make something to sell, whereas academic chemists are part of an international peer group; they are writing for each other. It may sound like I am denigrating that but I am not. I just want to make a distinction which I believe is very important for people in public policy to think about.

QUESTION: Yes, I would agree with that distinction. Would you be more comfortable if there was a presidential technology adviser rather than a science adviser?

MR. BILLINGTON: Yes.

QUESTION: Or would you prefer if Reagan got his Department of Technology and Science rather than Science and Technology?

MR. BILLINGTON: I am talking now historically about analysis. I am really not worried so much about prestige, about which name comes first.

It is a misnomer to talk about science in public policy, unless you mean how much money should be devoted to the support of scientific research for its own sake. If this is what you mean by science in public policy then that is an issue, an important issue, and I believe it should be addressed. But if you are talking about what I think most people mean by science in public policy, then I think it is a real misnomer.

QUESTION: Do you think it's just terminology or do you think there actually is too much money going to science?

MR. BILLINGTON: No, I think it is a misperception. For instance, in the early 1960s, IBM gave Harvard University a large grant to study technology and public policy. About one hundred people got together over a period of ten years. In that roster they did not list a single engineer, but it was called technology. They had a lot of scientists, perhaps because the image was that the scientists knew all about these issues and that the technologists were sort of following out the orders down below somewhere. The feeling may have been that you really did not have to talk to them because they are harder to talk to. Scientists seemed to get along much better in an academic community. They are happy to talk about these broader issues.

This program came out with publications which did not turn out to be very useful. I think the reason is because they never were talking about the real technological issues; they were talking theoretically in the least useful sense of the word.

QUESTION: Isn't there a contradiction here in the way it has developed, as you describe it? We are a highly pragmatic society. We want to get results from things, and even in philosophy we go back to William James and to Dewey and others. People argue that there must be some product. Even the "publish or perish" thing is an example of a product—getting something done—and yet here in this area the people with a product are disparaged.

From an intellectual history standpoint, how did this happen? Why is it that science has this prestige and technology, at least in the academy, may lack it? Is it because people, as you've just said, feel more at home with scientists? On the other hand, a number of marvelous people in chemistry and physics here really are interested only in a fairly narrow subject, so they don't discourse with a lot of the rest of us. There is some alienation among some scientists from the rest of the university. But do you have any hunch about how it occurred?

MR. BILLINGTON: Well, yes, I think I do. Hunch is the best word to use. I referred to the impact Einstein made when he came to this country and the impact he still makes on the imagination of the general public. From the point of view of the history of ideas that is a very important thing because he is somehow a saint. You should never underestimate what that means to the general culture, in particular to a general culture which has been pragmatic. And that pragmatism in the nineteenth century had, I think, a curious influence on our culture. Let me give you an example. If I were to mention the word railroads, nineteenth century railroads, and you did not know anything about the history of railroads, what kind of names would jump to mind? If I say, "The railroad expansion of the nineteenth century," whom would you think of?

QUESTION: Gould or Vanderbilt.

MR. BILLINGTON: See, you would never think of the engineers; you would think immediately of those barons. Now they were important, no doubt about it.

In Britain, if I would say railroads, 1825 to 1850, in other words when Britain dominated the world industrially, who would you think of? If you ask any Briton he will tell you instantly whom he would think of. He would think of George and his son Robert Stephenson and of I. K. Brunel, the engineers. They actually built the things. Now in some cases they financed them, but they were clearly engineers. Stevenson was really the founder of mechanical engineering.

Our society has tended to see these two poles around engineering. On the one side we have the Einsteins who represent the physical world in a certain way; on the other side we have the Hills and the Vanderbilts who represent the entrepreneurial side of technology.

Then what happened academically was that our pragmatism meant that engineering education in America was very pragmatic. I think it was very much oriented towards handbooks and practical things and not towards the more reflective, theoretical side of engineering. It had a wonderful influence in this country because engineering became a great place for upward mobility. You did not have to speak good English, so it meant a tremendous number of immigrants, who were bright people but who were not in higher society could go into engineering and could get excellent jobs.

I remember when I first came to Princeton in the early sixties, the dean of the Engineering School invited the headmaster of Exeter to come down and give a talk. The headmaster peered down and looked a little snobbish to us I think, and he said (as I recall it), "I'm really mystified why I am invited down here." He said, "I've been headmaster of Exeter for twenty-five years. It would never occur to me to advise any of our students ever to go into engineering. It just wouldn't occur to me."

On the Continent, engineering became something quite different. Those technological high schools were elite schools. People going to those schools felt that they were at the very top of society in every sense. They were being educated thoroughly and they were going out to become a cadre of people to restructure the world. There was a great emphasis on the fact that they were going to be an elite. In our society that was not the case, and I think for good reasons. It would probably have been wrong for us to treat the engineer in that way.

The Russian Revolution and then Hitler's time, both of those, sent to this country a tremendous number of these high-grade European engineers. And they made a great impact on our academies. Look at the names on the faculties all over the country and you will see it right away. I mean the most distinguished in our field was Stephan Timoshenko who came over and just revolutionized the teaching of civil and mechanical engineering because he brought with him a whole different tradition, a much higher tradition in an intellectual sense.

QUESTION: One thought I'm having as I listen to this is why the public doesn't perceive that. My perception of science always deals with medicine. When I think of scientists I think of Jonas Salk and of bio-medical research. To what extent does that blur the image of the scientist and the engineer in the public's eyes and confuse this whole question, and how does that complicate the issue?

MR. BILLINGTON: Everything complicates the issue. I think that agriculture and medicine are different questions. We might as well accept certain empirical facts. They are treated differently. I mean we have Schools of Agriculture and we have Schools of Medicine and we don't mix them in together with Arts and Sciences. I think they are separate issues and I think it is much better to keep them separate.

QUESTION: How do you do that in the public's eyes though? I don't understand the difference between what they do in research at the medical school and in biology and in chemistry departments. To me all these disciplines try to do the same thing. I don't understand what the difference is between what they teach at the chemistry department in the Engineering School and the chemistry department in the School of Arts and Sciences.

MR. BILLINGTON: I think that is a bona fide question and I think that it is up to the scientific and the engineering community to try to make that clear. Up to now they have not tried to do that. But it is just like in any other kind of subject. The culture has, over the past hundred years, made remarkable distinctions which the public finally is catching on to. We now know the difference between baroque and renaissance and rococo, which are terms invented relatively recently to try to explain to people certain differences. And I think we are coming to the time when we have to do this now in this area. It has to be done but you cannot do it when these things are all bubbling around. I mean you cannot go back and tell Bach that he is baroque. He would not have known what you meant. It would have been nonsense to him.

So I think that you have to wait. Now we have two hundred years of history behind us since the industrial revolution. That gives us a lot of time to ask these questions about differences and to observe empirically what has happened. Why do we have separate medical schools? Why are they not in biology departments? Why do some people do research in medical schools and other people do research in biology departments? Well, that is just an empirical fact. We better take that as a starting point. You cannot lump everybody together. It used to be that scientists were lumped under philosophy. They used to be natural philosophers. And then suddenly came a time when it no longer made sense to talk that way.

QUESTION: It seems to me that the questions are different in medicine and agriculture.

MR. BILLINGTON: Completely different questions, exactly. You have a different physical system you are worried about.

QUESTION: I was actually going to dispute that and say there are distinctions that don't become useful anymore. I would think that when they began medical schools they taught you diagnosis and they didn't have anything that they could usefully treat disease with. But they become more scientific. I am wondering if there comes a point when you shouldn't abandon distinctions.

MR. BILLINGTON: Well, maybe, but not yet. I think the first job is to make clear what people are doing right now or have been doing. You cannot predict the future. You do not know what things are going to evolve into. It is foolish to base your definitions on that. But I think it is sensible to say that over the past two hundred years certain things have happened. For instance, there is a mythology about medicine. There is a mythology that the introduction of drugs has been a major revolution in health care. Well again, historians have studied that problem and they find that they cannot justify that. They find that the diseases, the major diseases, have often been subjected to public health measures before they have been subjected to private health measures. The cleaning up of the water system does away with the need for most of the drugs. Now that is a very important perception that the public does not have. The public thinks that you need to pour money into research. There is a lot of evidence now that you should put money into cleaning up the air rather than focus only on cancer research. That is the kind of thing that you can demonstrate; that happened in nineteenth century England. When they cleared up smog, radical changes took place. There is evidence for things like that in the past.

But we do not want to believe that. We want to believe that pure scientific research in developing these things is going to be the answer. This is part of the mythology of science. That is why I would again come back to the public policy questions of air and water and things like that. We must get at the real source of our problems. There are so many elementary things that can be done. Again, it is the ideals of the engineer. It is to see things in terms of building something like a water treatment plant. Refined laboratory research by scientists can often help and both activities should clearly go on. The other is much more difficult to justify as a public issue.

QUESTION: If we ever cross the threshold from saying we need a science adviser to saying we need a technology adviser, what kind of profile could one draw? Given the business of government—environment, nuclear weapons, outer space—could one draw a profile of a single engineer who could oversee and keep an eye on all these different things?

MR. BILLINGTON: I do not think you have to have twenty-five advisers just because you can identify twenty-five different problems. I think that Guy Stever, for example, was knowledgeable; he had come from being president of an engineering school and he knew engineering in the broadest sense. I think someone like that was fine. In fact some of the scientists would be fine. But I do think that you need to have somebody who sees engineering in the broadest terms and who has some specialty, knows what research in engineering means, and knows what the actual putting into practice of some aspect of engineering also means. But I do not have any more specific profile than that.

I think the tendency was to get people who had been scientists and administrators. Not always, but by and large, and that is institutional diplomacy of how you go about these things probably is not a bad idea. I have not thought much about that.

QUESTION: But you could find that skill among engineers and technology people as well as among scientists?

MR. BILLINGTON: I think so. I think the man who ran Bell Labs, would be one example. The man who runs General Electric Labs is already head of the Science Advisory Committee now. So people like that are the kind of people you need, people who have some responsibility for overviewing lots of technological work. I think you do not necessarily want to get a practicing engineer but it does have to be somebody who has enough technical background to go fairly deeply in all these areas. Presidents want to have somebody who could sit down for a week and really become quite knowledgeable in any field. That would be an absolute prerequisite.

QUESTION: You made it clear that you think we need a technology adviser rather than a science adviser. Would that mean a different function or a different role as a technology adviser as opposed to a scientific adviser?

MR. BILLINGTON: I think the role would change. I think it would raise to a higher level the hard technological discussions. I mean there would be a lot of talk about the Star Wars Program. I heard a talk by an engineer from

MIT who had been in the federal government a long time as an adviser. He disliked Reagan and he disliked the whole idea of the Star Wars. But he made a very sensible discussion of it. He said (as I recall it), "There isn't any doubt, you have to do this because something out of that is going to work. We have to be there figuring out how it's going to work, what it's going to do. We have to be in it. We can't stay out of it." And that was a very impressive kind of presentation he made. It was a case of an engineer approaching it rather than a scientist—and an engineer who was thoroughly opposed to Reagan. He was not arguing as a supporter of the administration's proposal but just as an engineer trying to advise the country. He knew he was not going to learn anything about the universe from this work really. I mean, certainly there will be some things you will learn but that was not the idea. It was the making of something and the figuring out that appealed to him. To me it was a very convincing discussion. I could see that kind of a person as a technology adviser. Reagan would obviously never hire him!

QUESTION: That for example would almost be a normative question. But would that be the role of an adviser—to decide whether or not we can do it?

MR. BILLINGTON: Oh, I think it should be. I think the adviser should certainly not be neutral. There is nothing neutral about technology at all. You can not discuss it in any terms sensibly without taking a position. Science may be quite neutral but not technology.

QUESTION: So that would be one way the roles are changed.

MR. BILLINGTON: Yes.

QUESTION: Is a technologist any more likely to cross over the boundary of research? On strategic defense initiatives, deployment and production, would the habits of technology people lead them to be more likely to deploy than a basic scientist would? Or is the process just one which, whether it's technology or science, goes on automatically?

Herbert York used to argue that really you can't cut the thing off in terms of science. Once you've discovered something it already is on the procurement route so it really doesn't make any difference.

MR. BILLINGTON: Well, ideologically if you are talking about the difference between scientists and engineers, there's no doubt that for the engineer the working object is the thing that engages his attention. So if you think about the adviser as a technologist or engineer you are thinking of someone who conceives of things as working objects rather than as research programs. So there is a big difference there. I do not see how an engineer could think about any of those problems without thinking about production.

Now deployment is another issue. Maybe I do not understand how you use that term exactly. That seems to me to be a highly political issue. Or did you mean deployment in the sense of how they actually fire and how they actually go off?

QUESTION: Getting them out there and ready to fire.

MR. BILLINGTON: That is a political issue. I mean that is one where engineers' roles would I think stop. They would certainly have opinions about what should be built and what capabilities it would have rather than ideas of where it should be put and how it should be used. That seems to me to be so political.

QUESTION: How does a technology adviser in this sense reconcile what I see as two different roles. On the one hand, he is an advocate for technology. Yet he is the one who is supposed to be explaining what the limitations and the implications of technology are. It seems to me that oftentimes he would be at cross purposes there.

MR. BILLINGTON: Maybe I do not know enough about the role of the science adviser but I would think the science adviser has the same problem. I mean is that not implicit in any private adviser's role? If you want to get an expert, the person comes from a constituency which has certain lobbying functions, I suppose, and I would say that is just endemic in any problem. The best answer is to find someone who is an expert and who has integrity.

QUESTION: If we have a scientist though, who is alien to technology, is it easier for that scientist to deal with that question not having to go back at some point to his colleagues in technology?

MR. BILLINGTON: Well, if you want to argue from that point of view, then you might as well get an artist. If you get some painter who will go in there and advise on technology, obviously he does not have any axe to grind. No, I think the point of having a technology adviser is you want someone who is competent directly and who symbolizes as much as anything else what the real issues are, and does not confuse them as being issues of long-term basic, undirected research, which is what in a way the scientist symbolizes. Instead the engineer confronts the much more immediate issues that are continually confronting the government: immediate applications. We ought to recognize that the President needs to be advised by someone who certainly understands and can explain the question of production, the question of use—the question of physical use not the political use—on all of those things. And if you have somebody like Guy Stever in that position, there is a person who is not so kept by the technological establishment really. It is not as if you are getting the head of General Motors to come in and advise you about what kind of machines to make.

I think that a lot of the personal issues would be just as they are for anybody but I think the public issue would be much clearer. The general public would know that their President is being advised on the issues where so much of the money is going. That is really the whole point anyway, isn't it? So much of the money is going for all this hardware, all this technological stuff. So that is what the President needs advice on.

QUESTION: Are people in engineering or technology more likely to be closer to the so-called military industrial complex and therefore inclined— when they work in the national security area—to promote the production of new weapons?

MR. BILLINGTON: I think that since only part of engineering deals with the military industrial complex—the whole public works side does not deal with that—you have little to worry about there.

Now, clearly, if you are talking about someone coming from General Dynamics, there is obviously a close relationship, no doubt about it. There are large numbers of engineers, of course, who are involved in the industrial complex. I would like to feel that the technology advisers are really professional advisers and therefore are not kept by any such group one way or the other. I think that is the way the science advisers have been perceived.

NARRATOR: I think if we hadn't had this discussion, we would have a large missing chapter in our whole investigation of the science advisers.

CONCLUDING OBSERVATIONS

Kenneth W. Thompson

On few subjects of interest to the Miller Center have we found such unanimity on the importance of further study as on science advising. First, leaders of the University of Virginia science faculty have warmly supported the Center's efforts. This is particularly true of Dean and Commonwealth Professor Hugh Kelly of Physics and Professor Robert Kretsinger of Biology. Second, the Center has found the national science community no less encouraging. Not only the contributors to this small volume, but scholars such as Dean Don Price of Harvard, Professor Franklin Long of Cornell and former science adviser and university leader Guy Stever have called for continuing work by the Center. Finally, political scientists and historians are quick to point out that the president's science advising system deserves full and objective study by an objective source.

A former foundation colleague used to speak of making a particular area of inquiry one's parish. That is precisely what the Miller Center is contemplating. We hope that others will join us in this effort.

The stakes hardly need review. They include Star Wars, environmental deterioration, overpopulation, disease control, food production and arms control. With the best scientific knowledge, the challenge of these problems may prove overwhelming. Without good science advising, disaster on several fronts is not only possible but likely. But who is to advise, how is scientific advising to be organized, what can we say of past experience and what can we propose for the future?

Answers to such questions will not come easily. A few clues may emerge from these pages. If larger answers are anticipated even in part, they will come as a result of the kind of serious inquiry the participants in this volume challenge the Miller Center to undertake.